THE STRANGE DEATH OF AMERICAN
Liberalism

THE STRANGE DEATH OF AMERICAN
Liberalism

H. W. Brands

YALE UNIVERSITY PRESS

New Haven and London

Set in Carter Cone Galliard type by Keystone
Typesetting, Inc., Orwigsburg, Pennsylvania.
Printed in the United States of America.

Library of Congress Cataloging-in-Publication Data
Brands, H. W.
The strange death of American liberalism / H. W.
Brands.
    p. cm.
Includes bibliographical references and index.
ISBN 0-300-09021-8 (cloth : alk. paper)
    1. United States — Politics and government — 1945–1989.
2. Liberalism — United States — History — 20th century.
3. Political culture — United States — History — 20th
century. I. Title.
E743 .B68 2001
320.51′3′0973 — dc21   2001025867

A catalogue record for this book is available from the
British Library.

The paper in this book meets the guidelines for
permanence and durability of the Committee on
Production Guidelines for Book Longevity of the
Council on Library Resources.

10   9   8   7   6   5   4   3   2   1

CONTENTS

Preface *vii*

1 A Nation of Skeptics *1*

2 Beneath the Eagle's Wings *27*

3 The War That Never Ended *49*

4 Liberals All! *67*

5 From Hubris to Suttee *99*

6 The Contradictions of Cold War Conservatism *127*

7 Nunc Dimittis *153*

Afterword: The Lazarus Option *175*

Notes *179*

Sources *187*

Acknowledgments *191*

Index *193*

The unsolved mystery of American politics is: Who killed liberalism? The decease is undeniable (even if, like the passing of Elvis, it is occasionally denied). During the 1960s, liberalism permeated American political life; it was in the very air, supplying the optimism and energy that allowed Lyndon Johnson and the Great Society Congress to declare war on poverty and inequality and believe they could defeat those historic foes of human happiness. But by the mid-1970s the liberal dream had died, and by the early 1980s "liberal" had become an almost-actionable epithet. Subsequent sightings of liberalism's ghost were occasionally mistaken for the real thing, but after a feckless attempt by the first Clinton administration to refashion national health care, even the ghost was rarely seen.

Yet if liberalism is indubitably dead, much doubt surrounds the cause of death. Conservatives contend natural causes — not excluding the natural results of self-inflicted wounds. Liberalism, in this view, misread human nature, promised too much, and suffered the righteous wrath of a disillusioned electorate. Not so, reply liberals: the death was foul play. Liberalism was done in by its enemies, who pandered to the fears of a public alarmed by economic insecurity, itself largely the work of elites who managed to decouple their own fate from that of the masses increasingly left behind.

Each side adduces circumstantial evidence to bolster its case, but neither explanation gets to the heart of the matter. Liberalism has had a hundred definitions since the concept surfaced in England in the early nineteenth century; these have ranged from antimonarchical individualism to anticlerical secularism to antitrust progressivism to antinuclear environmentalism, from abolition to prohibition to states' rights to civil rights to human rights. There are economic liberals, social liberals, philosophical liberals; liberal realists, liberal idealists, liberal sentimentalists.

Predictably, liberals conceive liberalism differently than conservatives do. Liberals define themselves as defenders of the downtrodden against the rich and powerful, as upholders of equality in the face of inequality, as apostles of compassion and tolerance in a world distressingly devoid of both. Conservatives may or may not question liberals' motives, but they argue that the liberals' methods — typically centering on intervention by government — undermine the ends the liberals profess to desire. The welfare of ordinary men and women is best fostered, the conservatives contend, not by government but by those ordinary men and women themselves, if government simply stays out of their way.

A meaningful debate on any topic must commence with definitions acceptable to both sides. In the context of contemporary American politics, few of either liberals or conservatives would dispute that whatever else it entails, liberalism is premised on a prevailing confidence in the ability of government — preeminently the federal government — to accomplish substantial good on behalf of the American people. This confidence, abundantly evident during the 1960s, was what made possible the elaboration of the Great Society; the withdrawal of this confidence was what caused liberalism to wither and die.

Liberalism is dead, but liberals survive. This isn't a paradox, merely a consequence of the electoral arithmetic of American democracy. The difference between glorious victory and ignominious defeat is almost never more than two votes in ten, and those two unfailingly come from the fluid middle territory between convinced conservatives and determined liberals. Even in the heyday of LBJ, conservatives weren't hard to find—for instance, among the 39 percent who voted for Barry Goldwater. At the height of Ronald Reagan's conservative restoration, tens of millions of liberals, and 41 percent of voters, lined up behind Walter Mondale.

The critical consideration isn't what the zealots think but how far their thoughts influence the polity as a whole. In this regard the change between the 1960s and the late 1990s is unmistakable. During the 1960s the Johnson administration proposed, and Congress adopted, scores of ambitious and often expensive new federal programs; during the 1990s the trend was in just the opposite direction, with federal programs, often of long standing, regularly being dismantled, discontinued, or devolved to the states.

The connection between popular desires and political outcomes is rarely direct and never perfect; money and other forms of unequal influence skew the process. But it is fair to say—and public-opinion polls *do* say—that the anti-liberal sea change since the 1960s reflects a disenchantment among voters at large with the idea that government can accomplish much of benefit to them. Voters have adopted a stance of skepticism, in many cases outright hostility, regarding the expansion of government. They haven't insisted on rolling back every government program—not least because in their general skepticism many middle-class recipients of Social Security and other transfer payments have adopted an attitude of holding on to whatever they have. But they have stoutly, and successfully, resisted efforts to expand the scope of government.

The purpose of this book is to explain the demise of liberalism in terms of this withdrawal of popular confidence in government. The problem with nearly all post-liberal post mortems is that they lack historical perspective. The argument put forward here is that the liberalism that characterized the period from 1945 until the early 1970s was anomalous by the standards of American history. Moreover, this anomaly was chiefly the consequence of the predominant feature of global politics at the time — the Cold War. It states the matter only a bit too strongly to say that modern American liberalism was an artifact of the Cold War. It is *not* too much to say that without the Cold War, liberals would never have achieved the success they did. Nor is it too much to say that the collapse of the Cold War consensus in America was what doomed liberalism. Liberals lost not because they were wrong about American society, but because they were wrong about the world.

This argument may appear provocative, even perverse, in that it turns upside down conventional wisdom regarding the relative positions of domestic and international affairs in American politics. It is also likely to annoy many liberals by reminding them that the Cold War was originally their idea. But the point is that Cold War liberalism was a seamless conception of the nature of the world. Americans saw themselves locked in a global struggle with communism; this struggle was partly a matter of military power, but increasingly it became a struggle for the hearts and minds of the billions of people who would choose democracy or communism based on their perceptions as to which system was more likely to improve their lives. To defeat communism required powerful weapons; it also required the powerful example of a society that offered hope and opportunity to all.

Of equal importance, the Cold War fostered a mindset that

caused Americans to put aside their traditional distrust of big government and allow the public sector to grow at the expense of the private sphere. In this regard the Cold War was quite similar to each major war in American history, when the needs of national security had seemed to dictate an expansion of the powers and institutions of government. (As many others have noted—albeit usually with a different purpose—the Cold War wasn't called the Cold *War* for nothing.) Moreover, the peculiar nature of the Cold War amplified the normal wartime willingness to defer to Washington's judgment. Military secrets—now including nuclear secrets—were more sensitive than in any previous war. And because much of the Cold War was waged covertly, presidents depended on the willingness of Congress and the people not to inquire too closely into certain government activities. Finally, the very basis of American Cold War policy—the idea that a protracted containment of communism would lead to its eventual demise—was a proposition that had to be taken on faith.

For a generation the Cold War went well for the United States, and the popular trust in government the Cold War engendered seemed well placed. It was under this aegis of trust that the major reforms of the late 1950s, the 1960s, and the early 1970s took place, for even as the contest with communism appeared to make extra efforts to perfect American society necessary, the atmosphere of trust in government made them possible.

But then the Cold War went bad in Vietnam, and suddenly the official wisdom of a quarter-century didn't seem so wise anymore. And just as popular confidence in government had previously extrapolated from foreign affairs to domestic, so now did popular distrust. Americans who discovered that their leaders had been tragically wrong about Vietnam began to wonder whether those same leaders could have been right about anything. That Americans then learned that their leaders hadn't simply been wrong about Vietnam but had been persistently deceitful — and that the last Vietnam president, Richard Nixon, was the most deceitful of all — simply compounded the popular disillusionment with government.

Vietnam killed the American Cold War consensus, and in killing the Cold War consensus killed liberalism. Detente — the positive half of Nixon's legacy — represented an admission that the Cold War had become unsustainable on its original terms, and despite Reagan's anticommunist exhortations of the early 1980s, Americans never re-embraced the old containment gospel. Instead they reverted to their historic distrust of government, which Reagan encouraged at every opportunity — without appreciating that in doing so he was guaranteeing the failure of his simultaneous efforts to summon support for an activist foreign policy.

All this is of more than historical interest. If the argument of this book is correct — that the Cold War was a necessary precondition for the success of postwar liberalism — then the end of the Cold War would suggest that there isn't much hope for any imminent resurrection of liberalism. This is indeed the conclusion to be drawn. Americans traditionally are skeptics on the subject of government; absent compelling reason to look to Washington for solutions to their problems, they don't. They didn't before the Cold War (with exceptions explained in the chapters that follow); they haven't after the Cold War; and they won't until some new and comparable national emergency arises. Liberals can lament this, and doubtless will deny it; conservatives may applaud it, and likely will exaggerate it. But there it is.

A word about the scope of the present undertaking may be in order. This is by no means a history of American liberalism; far less is it a history of American political philosophy or political culture. It is, rather, an argument. The courteous reader will therefore forgive a certain argumentative tone and a deficiency of detail necessary to any comprehensive history but superfluous to the case put forward here. The author would not presume to dismiss counterarguments out of hand, but neither does he feel obliged to make them. That task he leaves to other books and other authors. The present objective is to outline an argument that, in the author's view, has received insufficient attention in debates over the watershed development of the last forty years in American politics.

THE STRANGE DEATH OF AMERICAN
Liberalism

1

A NATION OF SKEPTICS

Americans who came of age after 1945 might have been forgiven for assuming liberalism was the norm in American politics. From the New Deal through the Cold War, there was indeed a liberal bias in American thinking about the relation of government to people. But in the overall scheme of American history, this liberalism was anomalous. From before they had become a nation, and continuing until almost the middle of the twentieth century, Americans registered chronic skepticism regarding a more active role for the federal government in their lives. Every generation harbored its advocates of activism, but every generation comprised a larger collection of skeptics.

THRIVING ON NEGLECT

Distrust of government came over on some of the first ships from England. The Pilgrims and Puritans who settled New England did so explicitly to escape the arm of Anglican law, and they were followed shortly by Catholics, Quakers, and dissenters of other stripes.

Once established in America, these and their colonist kin grew accustomed to having their own way in secular matters as well. London legislated for the colonies, for instance on trade and manufactures, but London was far away and for most of the colonial period contented itself with Walpole's famous "salutary neglect." Imperial prohibitions didn't prevent the colonists from smuggling molasses, forging nails, or doing a hundred other things nominally proscribed to them.

It was precisely Parliament's belated effort to remedy this neglect that set in motion the events leading to the American Revolution, for the colonists considered the Sugar, Stamp, Tea, and related acts not remedies but just the opposite. When they vowed "no taxation without representation," it wasn't the representation they wanted (they rejected Charles Townshend's offer of same) but the taxation they did *not* want. Thomas Paine's *Common Sense* and Thomas Jefferson's Declaration of Independence were chiefly indictments of the overweening power of the British imperial government.

The Revolutionary War itself revealed the depth of American distrust of centralized authority—even when that authority was their own. George Washington was repeatedly driven to distraction (and almost to resignation) by the refusal of a jealous Continental Congress to grant him the wherewithal to prosecute the war effectively, and by the refusal of the states to supply what the Congress did requisition. Many, probably most, Americans of revolutionary bent believed Providence smiled on their cause; that their side won in spite of its hobbled leadership appeared additional evidence of divine favor (and of George Washington's greatness).

To guarantee that they not simply resaddle themselves with despotism, Americans in most states insisted on attaching bills of rights to their state constitutions. The concept came from English history, dating to Magna Carta; the purpose, as articulated in the instructions of the Virginia voters of Albermarle County to their delegates to the state's constitutional convention, was to draw "a proper and clear line . . . between the powers necessary to be conferred by the Constituents to their delegates, and what ought prudently to remain in their hands."[1]

When the difficulties of fighting a war and managing a peace convinced many Americans that the Articles of Confederation required replacement by something stronger, the most vigorous advocates of a federal government denied that the new national charter needed a bill of rights. If Alexander Hamilton, James Madison, and the other Federalists were to be believed, the very nature of the new government—as the careful creation of the American people, endowed with only those powers expressly delineated in the Constitution—rendered a bill of rights unnecessary. "For why declare that things shall not be which there is no power to do?" asked Hamilton disarmingly.[2]

In point of fact, most Americans did *not* believe Hamilton and the others. Although a working majority were willing to accept a stronger government, they were not about to do so without explicit hedges on the powers of that government. "Why was not the Constitution ushered in with the bill of rights?" demanded James Lincoln of South Carolina. "Are the people to have no rights?" Luther Martin of Maryland thought he knew the answer to Lincoln's question. Speaking of the framers of the proposed federal government, Martin warned, "Their object is the total abolition and destruction of all state governments, and the erection on their ruins of one great and extensive empire, calculated to aggrandize and elevate its rulers and chief officers far above the common herd of mankind."[3]

The upsurge of skepticism forced the Federalists to retreat and accept a bill of rights as the price of ratification — a price that subsequently diminished somewhat when one of their own, Madison, assumed charge of drafting the promised guarantees.

In 1789 Madison held his nose at what he called "the nauseous project of amendments": within less than a decade he decided that the amendments weren't so stomach-turning after all. Now a Republican and an opponent of the Federalist administration of John Adams, Madison joined Jefferson in opposing the Sedition Act of 1798 as a violation of the First Amendment — besides being odious on its merits. Madison quietly penned a resolution by which the Republican-controlled Virginia legislature denounced the Federalist usurpation (including the companion Alien Act); Jefferson did likewise for Kentucky.[4]

The small-government Republicans succeeded in displacing the Federalists in the elections of 1800, causing Jefferson, in his inaugural address, to reaffirm his commitment to "a wise and frugal government which shall restrain men from injuring one another, shall leave them otherwise free to regulate their own pursuits of industry and improvement, and shall not take from the mouth of labor the bread it has earned." In this same address Jefferson said Americans were "all Republicans and all Federalists," which not surprisingly raised doubts in his listeners, both among Republicans who hoped he was fibbing and among Federalists who were sure he was. Subsequent actions suggested that his continued devotion to minimal government was likewise at least partly rhetorical. Jefferson was hardly the last president to discover that power wasn't half as bad when wielded by oneself as it had been in the hands of those rascals who went before. He swallowed his strict-constructionist principles to purchase Louisiana and extended the reach of government to breathtaking — specifically, transoceanic — distances in engineering the embargo of American commerce with Britain and France.[5]

Even those Republican loyalists who loved nearly everything Jefferson did had difficulty endorsing such a sweeping assertion of federal power, and Jefferson left office to the jeers of his enemies and the embarrassed silence of many of his friends. The war his embargo foreshadowed was the most controversial foreign conflict in the nation's history (more controversial than the Vietnam War, which even at its most divisive didn't provoke the serious talk of secession the War of 1812 did, except in such epicenters of activist symbolism as the People's Republics of Madison, Wisconsin — what must Jemmy's ghost have been thinking? — and Berkeley, California, and then only with tongue-in-chic).

The "era of good feelings" that followed the War of 1812 felt good chiefly by comparison with the decades of dispute that preceded and followed it. A continuing concern of Westerners like Henry Clay of Kentucky was the desirability of federal support for infrastructure development — "internal improvements," as they were called. Clay dressed his designs for federal funding of roads in the language of an "American system," which also embraced a national bank and a tariff to bar imports that competed with American products. Clay found a majority (mostly among those refugee Federalists who were following him into the Whig party) for a protective tariff; likewise for a second Bank of the United States. But federal road building foundered on the apathy of the East (which already had most of the roads it needed) toward projects that would principally benefit the West, and on a lingering conception that something so geographically specific ought to be left to the states. Appropriately for anything with Clay's name on it, a compromise was struck:

Congress funded the National Road (as the main interstate highway from Baltimore to — eventually — Vandalia, Illinois, was called) but, facing opposition from Presidents Madison and Monroe, ignored most of the rest of Clay's infrastructure program.

Clay's centralizing vision received still rougher treatment from Andrew Jackson. Clay brought his troubles upon himself by persuading the director of the Bank of the United States, Nicholas Biddle, to apply for early recharter in 1832; Jackson, up for reelection, accepted the challenge and made the bank the centerpiece of his campaign. To the Jacksonians the bank represented an unwarranted and dangerous usurpation by the federal government (in league with the hated Eastern money men) of prerogatives legitimately reserved to the states. Jackson vowed to return power to its rightful place. "The bank, Mr. Van Buren, is trying to kill me," Old Hickory told his protégé and eventual successor. "But I will kill it!" He proceeded to do just that, first by veto of the recharter, second by winning reelection, and third by the transfer of federal funds from the national bank to state banks.[6]

The French observer Alexis de Tocqueville happened to be in America during Jackson's assault on the bank, and he was struck by what this and other contemporary events said about Americans' preference for a weak central government. "The prominent feature of the administration in the United States," Tocqueville observed, "is its excessive decentralization." The preference for local control had "been carried farther than any European nation could endure without great inconvenience."

Tocqueville took pains to distinguish between *government*, by which he meant the potential or constitutional scope of federal power, and *administration*, the actual exercise of day-to-day control. Of the former the United States had no dearth. "It would be easy to prove that the national power is more concentrated there than it has ever been in the old nations of Europe." This simply made the exceedingly modest scope of federal administration more remarkable. "In the American republics the central government has never as yet busied itself except with a small number of objects, sufficiently prominent to attract its attention. The secondary affairs of society have never been regulated by its authority; and nothing has hitherto betrayed its desire of even interfering in them."[7]

THESE UNITED STATES

As Tocqueville noticed and Jackson demonstrated, in those relatively few areas of life where Americans of the eighteenth and nineteenth centuries admitted the need for active government, they greatly preferred that the government doing the acting be a state government rather than the federal government. Until the Civil War, of course, there existed a lively — ultimately deadly — debate over which level of government held sovereign priority. One version of the states' rights argument countenanced nullification: the denial of legitimacy within a given state to a federal law deemed obnoxious. This was Jefferson and Madison's position in the Kentucky and Virginia resolutions; it was also the position of South Carolinians who refused to enforce the 1828 tariff (the "tariff of abominations," they and their friends called it). Jackson, by threatening to hang the South Carolina nullifiers, demonstrated that an advocate of small government could simultaneously be a unionist.

The Civil War settled the issue of states' rights versus federal authority, but only in the constitutional sense. The federal government *could* overrule the states; the question remained whether it *should*. (This was the distinction Tocqueville had drawn in observing that it rarely did.) The new Republican party, emboldened by its own audacity in fighting to preserve the Union — and aided by the secessionary departure of the Southern Democrats — said yes on such matters of legislation as a transcontinental railroad and the dedication of a small part of the public domain to the support of higher education, and on the constitutional adjustments that were supposed to secure the fruits of victory in the Civil War. Yet if the Republicans were the party of Union, they were also the party of business, and while they were delighted to enact measures that facilitated the expansion of American capitalism, they had no desire to create costly new programs that would require raising taxes. What they couldn't fund through the tariff and the sale of public lands, they didn't deem worth doing, and consequently left undone. And in any event, the post-Reconstruction return of the Democrats put a check on Republican ambitions. (In addition, the Republican wartime program was a *wartime* program, of which more later.)

Through the end of the nineteenth century the states remained the focus of political activity in America. Incorporating industrialists looked to the state governments for charters, franchises, and other necessities of business life. The additional attraction of state government, as against the federal government, was that state legislatures were easier to buy, when purchase became necessary, than Congress. (The lagniappe of working with the state legislatures in those pre-Seventeenth Amendment days was that it conferred control over a state's U.S. senators.)

One measure of the relative lack of interest in the federal government during the last decades of the nineteenth century was the decidedly undistinguished character of the individuals who went into national politics. Of the post-Lincoln, pre-Theodore Roosevelt pres-

idents, none sticks in historical memory; the one who comes closest—William McKinley—does so by fortuitous virtue of presiding
over a war he initially opposed. Congress was even more forgettable
than the presidency. With the exception of House Speaker Thomas
Reed of Maine, who regularly paralyzed opponents in the golden
amber of his wit and who single-handedly revolutionized the rules
of the lower chamber, there were no members of Congress who
could have carried Daniel Webster's law books, tied Henry Clay's
cravat, or sharpened John Calhoun's quill pen. Not that the gifted
individuals were flocking to state government either—instead they
were busy becoming Andrew Carnegie, John D. Rockefeller, and
J. P. Morgan.

THE FAILURE OF POPULISM AND
THE MEANING OF PROGRESSIVISM

That was precisely what worried Ignatius Donnelly, Mary Lease,
and the other founders of the People's Party of the 1890s. The Populists were the first group to seriously challenge the new political
economy of the industrial age. The mythology of the movement
stood in a long line of American looniness; the black-helicopter
spotters of the 1990s were the direct ideological, and doubtless in
some cases biological, descendants of those many Populists who
were convinced that the Rothschilds held the world in the palms of
their grasping, and not coincidentally Jewish, hands. But the Populists' platform was hard-headed enough. They wanted the federal
government to devalue the currency, to nationalize the railroads and
telephone and telegraph lines, to seize land held by railroads and
other corporations in excess of actual use, to redistribute wealth

through a graduated income tax, to market crops for farmers, and to shorten the workday for industrial laborers. "We believe," they stated by way of summary in their 1892 platform, "that the powers of government — in other words, of the people — should be expanded . . . as rapidly and as far as the good sense of an intelligent people and the teachings of experience shall justify, to the end that oppression, injustice, and poverty shall eventually cease in the land."[8]

It was a breathtaking program, and one that American voters decisively rejected in 1896. William Jennings Bryan and the Democrats didn't steal the whole Populist program, but even free silver — essentially a scam by which Washington would engineer massive across-the-board price hikes that would relieve debt-strapped farmers — was sufficient to frighten that resounding majority that chose McKinley and the status-quo Republicans over Bryan and his Democratic-Populist coalition.

Yet the problems the Populists identified didn't disappear with McKinley's election. (Actually, two did: Grover Cleveland's depression gave way to a McKinley recovery, and fresh discoveries of gold in South Africa and the Yukon, and better techniques of refining gold ore, expanded the currency in a way that rendered silver superfluous.) After the turn of the century a new coalition of reformers recycled parts of the Populist agenda. The progressives — both those who joined the party of that name in 1912 and the many more Republicans and Democrats who held similar views but stuck with their old parties — followed the Populists in advocating a larger role for government. Progressivism surfaced at the national level after years of bubbling up from the cities and the states. Reformers attacking municipal corruption often found themselves trumped in the statehouses; to fix the former required repairing the latter. Likewise state reformers trying to rein in the trusts found themselves stymied by the commerce clause of the Constitution, which reserved such power to the federal government; to save the states demanded going federal.

If the logic of the American system pushed the progressives toward federal politics, so did the psychologic of certain progressive leaders. Theodore Roosevelt thirsted for power, not entirely for its own sake but also for what it allowed him to accomplish toward what he deemed worthy goals. Roosevelt had been tilting against the trusts and the bosses since his time in the New York assembly, and he spent six years during the late 1880s and early 1890s implementing the Pendleton Act and related reforms as a federal Civil Service commissioner. When fate — in the form of McKinley's assassination — made him president in 1901, progressivism suddenly had a champion at the apex of the federal government, one who intended to make the most of his position atop that pinnacle.

Roosevelt's reforms included the first meaningful enforcement of the Sherman antitrust act of 1890; he shocked the corporate world in 1902 when he announced prosecution of the J. P. Morgan-organized Northern Securities railroad trust. Morgan went to the White House to demand to know why the president was making such a fuss. "If we have done anything wrong," the financier said, "send your man to my man and they can fix it up." Roosevelt replied, "That can't be done." Roosevelt's point was that the days of the bosses' fixing things up were over. "We don't want to fix it up," explained Attorney General Philander Knox. "We want to stop it."[9]

Roosevelt followed his triumph in antitrust (which the Supreme Court obligingly ratified in 1906) with legislation that strengthened federal oversight of railroads. The Elkins Act of 1903 was largely toothless, but the Hepburn Act of 1906 established enforceable schedules of maximum charges and cognate standards of corporate good behavior. In other areas as well, Roosevelt extended the reach of Washington. After Upton Sinclair caused national indigestion with *The Jungle,* his indictment of the meat-packing trade, Roosevelt and the president's progressive allies in Congress pushed through the Pure Food and Drug Act of 1906.

In still other areas Roosevelt didn't need the help of Congress. By executive fiat he placed millions of acres of federal land into forest reserves (later called national forests), where they would be beyond the reach of the most rapacious cut-and-run timber interests. On a smaller scale he enlarged the nation's game reserves — partly out of concern for the wildlife therein, partly out of fear that hunters like himself would someday want for targets.

Compared to what had gone before, the years of Roosevelt's presidency were indeed an age of federal assertiveness. But not even TR, speaking from his bully pulpit, was able to overcome the inertia of popular skepticism regarding Washington's intentions. Republican regulars had from the first resisted Roosevelt's efforts to draw power to the White House, and by the end of his second (first full) term, he had a regular revolt on his hands. His last great effort on behalf of conservation came in the waning moments before a midnight withdrawal of federal forests from executive control; at that eleventh hour he and Gifford Pinchot were on hands and knees on maps spread out across the floor of Roosevelt's office, claiming this parcel and that tract, then that and that and that, before his authority expired.

Although he might have seen this insurrection as a portent, Roosevelt left office thinking reform was safe in the hands of William Howard Taft. But Taft, by temperament a judge rather than an executive, lacked Roosevelt's confidence in the capacity of government

to fix what ailed America. Taft continued to pursue antitrust viola-
tors, yet in other respects he was happy for private interests to regain
ground they had lost under Roosevelt.

What made Taft happy infuriated Roosevelt, who returned from
safari in Africa to rally the forces of reform against his heir. Roosevelt was clearly the more popular of the two; in primary elections
(a progressive reform just taking hold in the spring of 1912) he
trounced Taft, who in turn carried most of the party caucuses. These
latter victories revealed Taft's continuing grip on the party machinery, which duly delivered him the nomination that summer.

Roosevelt's resulting Bull Moose bolt delighted Democrats even
as it rankled Republicans; the party of Jefferson and Jackson looked
likely to elect a president for the first time since 1892. Progressives
felt torn by the need to choose between Roosevelt and the Democratic nominee, the progressive governor of New Jersey, Woodrow
Wilson; but many simultaneously took encouragement from the
near-certainty that one of the two progressive challengers would
displace the conservative incumbent.

As Taft fell back in the autumn race, an important distinction
surfaced between Roosevelt's and Wilson's brands of progressivism.
All the progressives recited the mantra of democracy in stating their
case for reform; government must act to restore the balance between
business interests and the American people that had been upset by
industrialization. But where Roosevelt would restore the balance at
the enlarged level of big business by strengthening government,
Wilson proposed to restore the balance at the historic lower level of
the people by weakening business.

Roosevelt's program borrowed from the work of Herbert Croly,
who in *The Promise of American Life* espoused marrying Hamiltonian
activism to Jeffersonian individualism — while acknowledging that

the union "will necessarily do more harm to the Jeffersonian group of political ideas than it will to the Hamiltonian." With Croly, Roosevelt accepted that modernization had changed forever the terms on which public and private interests would interact. The age of industry was the age of consolidation; small enterprises had consolidated into large enterprises, with benefits to the American standard of living that were obvious daily. At the same time, consolidation allowed America to keep pace with the other great nations in an age of global competition. "If we are to compete with other nations in the markets of the world," Roosevelt told the Progressive nominating convention in August 1912, "as well as to develop our own material civilization at home, we must utilize those forms of industrial organization that are indispensable to the highest industrial productivity and efficiency." In the same speech Roosevelt approvingly quoted from a recent work by Charles Van Hise of the University of Wisconsin, in which the reformist author cited the three C's of centralizing progressivism: concentration, cooperation, and control. "Through concentration we may have the economic advantages coming from magnitude of operations," Roosevelt repeated from Van Hise. "Through cooperation we may limit the wastes of the competitive system. Through control by commission we may secure freedom for fair competition, elimination of unfair practices, conservation of our natural resources, fair wages, good social conditions, and reasonable prices." Lest any confusion cloud his auditors' understanding, Roosevelt stated in his own voice just what he had in mind. "A national industrial commission should be created which should have complete power to regulate and control all the great industrial concerns engaged in interstate business — which practically means all of them in this country."[10]

Wilson, at least before becoming president, was less comfortable with power than Roosevelt. In keeping with the fact that he was of the party of Jefferson—a predecessor Roosevelt despised on partisan, historical, and philosophical grounds—Wilson refused to relinquish the Jeffersonian ideal of a nation of yeoman farmers and small merchants. Wilson wouldn't accept that government must grow until it could match the strength of the industrial trusts; he believed that the people were entirely within their rights and competence to bring industry back down to a pre-behemoth level where competition would resume and individual opportunity would revive. Nor did Wilson have Roosevelt's faith in the beneficence of bigness, even in the narrow realm of business itself. The great trusts were ungainly giants that had achieved their preeminence not by doing better what all businesses should aspire to do—that is, deliver quality products to willing customers at fair prices—but precisely by preventing others from doing that. Their bad consciences were revealed in their constant fear that some small outfit—a pygmy by comparison—would break their monopolies.

This was exactly what Wilson advocated. "For my part, I want the pigmy to have a chance to come out. And I foresee a time when the pigmies will be so much more athletic, so much more astute, so much more active, than the giants, that it will be a case of Jack the giant-killer. Just let some of the youngsters I know have a chance and they'll give these gentlemen points."

Wilson ridiculed Roosevelt's assertion that government should, or could, tame the beast by tackling it on its own turf. In principle this was simply wrong. "Shall we withhold our hand and say monopoly is inevitable, that all we can do is to regulate it? Shall we say that all that we can do is to put government in competition with monopoly and try its strength against it? . . . Have we come to a time when the President of the United States or any man who wishes to be the President must doff his cap in the presence of this high finance, and say, 'You are our inevitable master, but we will see how we can make the best of it'?"

And the practice would be worse than the principle. "If the government is to tell big business men how to run their business, then don't you see that big business men have to get closer to the government even than they are now? Don't you see that they must capture the government, in order not to be restrained too much by it?" Indeed, Wilson discerned evidence that business had already infiltrated government. The question for the American people was very simple: "Are you going to own your own premises, or are you not?"[11]

Of course the election wasn't really as simple as that, and other issues blurred the picture, as they always do. The split in the Republican party gave Wilson an important edge on his opponents; at the same time, Roosevelt's huge reputation — following a triumphal tour of the courts of Europe, he might well have been the most famous man in the world — amplified the Rough Rider's voice.

Even so, in the closest approximation the American people had yet had to a referendum on the question of big government versus small government in the new industrial age, they went decisively with Wilson. Wilson garnered only 42 percent of the popular vote in the three-way race, but this was half again as much as runner-up Roosevelt. The American people wanted reform but not more government.

What they got wasn't so easy to characterize. Like Jefferson a century earlier, President Wilson found power more tempting than

Candidate Wilson had. The principal reforms of his first two years mixed Roosevelt's stump thinking with his own. In good Democratic tradition he engineered a reduction of the tariff, which lessened the weight of government's thumb in the scales of marketplace. He presided over the institution of a small income tax, which did the opposite. The creation of the Federal Reserve System tended toward centralization, but the makeup of the system's board of governors and their relative independence from Congress and the executive made it almost an adjunct of the private banking system rather than of government. The Federal Trade Commission, a permanent agency established to ensure fair trade practices, could have come right out of Croly.

Where Wilson would have gone next, and how the American people would have responded, became confused at this point by the outbreak of the war in Europe. Although the war itself required more than two years to reach America, it distracted both president and people and tended to dissipate the reforming spirit. Congress did approve laws barring child labor and easing farmers' access to credit, but the latter was short corn and low cotton next to what the Plains and Dixie had been demanding for a generation, and the former hardly dented the problems that organized labor was having with immigrants and other low-wage workers. (The war, by increasing demand and cutting off most emigration from Europe, accomplished far more to improve the lot of workers than anything Washington did.)

By the time the war eclipsed domestic reform as the critical issue with American voters, it was possible to render a verdict on what progressivism meant and what it had accomplished. Certain new structures did indeed extend the powers of Washington. The

Newlands Act made Washington the chief irrigator and flood controller of the West; the Internal Revenue Service dipped into the wallets of the wealthy; the Federal Reserve maintained the stability of the currency, or tried to; the Federal Trade Commission put the fear of the feds into businessmen bent on collusion.

But in the grand scheme of things, the most noticeable achievements of the progressives were either procedural or negative. The direct election of senators and (in those states that adopted them) primary elections and the initiative, referendum, and recall might have been—and were—said to improve the functioning of democracy, but they did nothing to expand the scope of government. Those reforms that *did* broaden government's powers were chiefly intended to curtail wrongdoing of a sort that hadn't occurred to anyone to curtail before the onset of industrialism. Trusts were new, and antitrust measures were essentially an extension of the law codes that had defined fair business practice for centuries. Regulation of railroads fell into the same category: an old principle updated for fresh circumstances. With the passing of the frontier and the application of industrial processes to logging and mining, the once-limitless resources of the nation required new protection—but of the sort that had guarded the commons in English villages since time out of mind.

What the progressives—even such relative radicals as Roosevelt in his Bull Moose incarnation—essentially lacked was a *positive* conception of government. They laid the basis for a regulatory state, one invested with greater police powers than before. But almost none of them—at least not those of political heft—had even a glimmering of what would characterize modern liberalism: a state where government didn't simply prevent evil but actively promoted good.

CONSERVATIVE TRIAGE

Roosevelt likely would have been elected president in 1920 had he lived that long. In his fury at Wilson for the president's slowness to go to war against Germany—a fury personalized by Wilson's refusal, once he did pick up the gage, to let Roosevelt lead a division of volunteers to France—the apostate of 1912 returned to the fold of Republican regularity. After two consecutive losses—something the Republicans had never previously experienced in their entire existence as a party—the regulars would have nominated the devil if he could have delivered the White House. Roosevelt beat the devil, although not by much in the opinion of many mossbacks. Moreover, as the voters had demonstrated in rebuking Wilson in the congressional races of 1918, Americans were tired of Democratic crusades. The outcome of the peace conference—the flawed Versailles treaty—made them wearier still.

Yet it was just as well that Roosevelt died in 1919, for the end of the war revealed that the country was in a profoundly unprogressive mood. Some disputed Warren Harding's spelling of "normalcy," but almost no one contested its definition: a retreat from the reformism of the Progressive era and the global do-gooding of the war to the private and local concerns that had always typified American attitudes. When Calvin Coolidge said America's business was business, he meant that government ought to get out of the way and let businessmen do what they did, more or less unhindered by government bureaucrats. Businessmen weren't above accepting help overseas: Herbert Hoover's Commerce Department became a business ministry abroad. But at home the mood was more hostile to governmental activism than it had been for a generation. While Hoover's best-selling *American Individualism* was actually more sophisticated than readers might have guessed from the title and from the author's orphan-to-millionaire background, the title did fairly capture his voluntaristic philosophy, which in turn captured the American zeitgeist.

It did, at any rate, until the stock market crashed and the Great Depression set in. The hard times didn't change Hoover's approach; he continued to cling to the idea that individuals must look out for themselves and that the primary objective of government is to live within its means. Voters almost certainly would have agreed if Hoover's approach had worked. But when the third anniversary of Black Thursday came around just two weeks before the 1932 election with the economy still seeking bottom, voters not unreasonably decided to try something else.

Precisely what they were trying in electing Franklin Roosevelt was impossible to say with any assurance. Roosevelt's foremost qualification was that he wasn't Hoover, but from his speeches voters could be forgiven for confusing the two. Roosevelt lashed the Republicans for being "committed to the idea that we ought to center control of everything in Washington," and he vowed to cut federal expenditures by 25 percent. "I accuse the present Administration of being the greatest spending Administration in peace times in all our history. It is an Administration that has piled bureau on bureau, commission on commission."[12]

Whether or not Roosevelt sincerely intended to reduce the size and intrusiveness of government, he certainly intended to give that impression — which, for the purpose of the present argument, is more significant. Roosevelt recognized that while American voters wanted an end to the depression, they weren't clamoring for bigger government.

And indeed, the striking thing about the New Deal is how limited it actually was, considering the extent of the calamity the country was facing at the time. Roosevelt resisted demands from leftover Populists and hard-core progressives that he nationalize the fast-dissolving banking system; instead he opted for reorganization and new regulations that left ownership and control squarely in the private sector. The securities industry — in many minds the chief culprit in the stock market crash and the progenitor of most of the suffering that followed — likewise was merely regulated more tightly than before.

Not all the New Deal programs were so circumspect. Roosevelt's farm program *did* signify a departure, and in a decidedly liberal direction. Forty years after the Populists had called for government to become the market-clearing purchaser of last resort, the Agriculture Adjustment Act essentially accomplished that goal.

The National Recovery Administration was even more ambitious. Four years after the crash, with the economy floundering as helplessly as ever, the NRA was designed to provide the leadership and direction so obviously lacking on the private sector's own. Under federal supervision, major manufacturers, big labor, and such customers as were well organized would get together to devise codes of cooperative conduct. On the apparently unarguable premise that there wasn't enough demand to go around, the NRA codes placed government in the position of referee between erstwhile competitors for the demand that did exist.

Problems developed at once, however. Roosevelt recognized that anything as intrusive as the NRA was a huge stretch for Americans, even amid the current crisis; to minimize the possibility of injury to the popular psyche (and hence his own administration), he settled for voluntary compliance rather than federal mandates. But at a moment when thousands of firms were fighting for their lives, compliance came hard, and the codes began to break down even before they were put in place. Contributing to this breakdown was the fact that although some of the largest businesses judged that they could live with what amounted to government-supervised cartels, their smaller competitors feared being ground to bits between the millstones of a command economy.

The Supreme Court sided with the critics. In the 1935 *Schechter* case it tossed out the NRA, dealing a body blow to the whole concept of central planning. Further damage followed the Court's overruling of related New Deal measures.

Roosevelt plotted a counterattack, and after his rousing reelection in 1936 he unveiled a plan for liberalizing the Court. Actually, he didn't unveil it so much as try to keep it veiled by couching his scheme in the language of lightening the workload of the overburdened justices.

The disguise fooled no one, however, and the reaction against his Court-packing plan constituted the sharpest reverse Roosevelt ever suffered. Indeed, by some persuasive interpretations, it marked the beginning of the end of the New Deal. The surprising thing about the opposition to Roosevelt's Court plan was the broad spectrum from which it emanated. Conservatives were outraged, of course, because it was a conservative Court that was under attack. But even many of those who supported Roosevelt on the merits of the New Deal programs he wanted to preserve (or reinstate) worried about what such a manipulation of the judiciary by the executive might foreshadow. The old Bull Mooser William Allen White warned: "Assuming, which is not at all impossible, a reactionary president, as charming, as eloquent and as irresistible as Roosevelt, with power to change the court, and we should be in the devil's own fix if he decided to abridge the bill of rights by legislation which he could easily call emergency legislation."[13]

White's premise appeared particularly possible at the time, and it was this as much as anything Roosevelt himself did that made the specter of an out-of-control executive seem so alarming to so many people. With democracy losing its grip in Europe and with such homegrown demagogues as Huey Long and Charles Coughlin crowding the headlines and radio receivers of America, Roosevelt's attempt to undermine judicial independence could easily be interpreted as part of a concerted power grab. In rejecting Roosevelt's Court-packing plan, Americans registered their concern at the growing power of the federal government.

Not, by any means, that they rejected every manifestation of that growing power. The New Deal program that had the largest and longest-lasting impact was the Social Security system. Other income-maintenance programs, such as the various jobs schemes of the Civilian Conservation Corps, the Works Progress Administration, and the Public Works Administration, were intentionally temporary: short-term responses to current record unemployment and growing despair. The farm program established under the Agriculture Adjustment Act targeted a specific sector of the economy. But Social Security would touch every sector and eventually almost everybody.

Yet even in embracing the concept of collective responsibility for preventing old-age penury, Roosevelt did so most modestly (initial pensions started at ten dollars per month) and in a way that minimized the collectiveness of that responsibility. Where other countries paid pensions out of general government revenues, the American Social Security system was set up on the model of private insurance programs, with individual benefits keyed to individual contributions. The government might be the broker, but individuals paid the premiums for themselves and their families.

Roosevelt understood exactly what he was doing in designing the system so. "If I have anything to say about it" — and of course no one had more to say about it than he did — "it will always be contributed, and I prefer it to be contributed, both on the part of the employer and the employee, on a sound actuarial basis. It means no money out of the Treasury." In a moment of particular candor he told a critic who complained that the tax on employees diminished the efficiency and equity of the system: "I guess you're right on the economics, but those taxes were never a problem of economics. They are politics all the way through. We put those payroll contributions there so as to give the contributors a legal, moral, and political right to collect their pensions and their unemployment benefits. With those taxes in there, no damn politician can ever scrap my social security program."[14]

Roosevelt's appreciation of Americans' continuing skepticism toward big government was largely instinctive; he played politics by ear. But during this same period trained experts were learning to read music. Scientific polling began during the 1930s, supplanting the impressionistic sampling done as a sideline by such journals as the *Literary Digest*. The Gallup poll, which commenced surveying in 1935, gained credibility when it correctly called the 1936 Roosevelt-Landon contest — a race the *Literary Digest* got wildly wrong.

In its initial poll, conducted in September 1935, Gallup asked whether Americans thought the amount the government spent on relief and recovery was too little, too great, or about right. Twice as many respondents said spending was too great as declared it about right; less than one out of ten deemed it too little. In December of the same year voters were asked to name the most vital issue facing the country. Employment ranked first, which was hardly shocking at a moment when the unemployed numbered more than 8 million; second was economy in government. Tax reduction came in fourth, following neutrality in foreign affairs.

This concern with overgrown government persisted through the end of the decade. A poll taken over the New Year's holiday at the beginning of 1936 showed 70 percent of respondents declaring that it was necessary to balance the federal budget and start reducing the national debt. After Roosevelt's reelection, even among Democrats 50 percent of voters hoped his second administration would be more conservative than his first, as against 19 percent who wanted it to be more liberal and 31 percent who wanted it to be about the same. Among Republicans 88 percent wanted it to be more conservative. A survey taken in June 1938 asked the same question but omitted the "about the same" answer; among voters at large 72 percent said "more conservative" and only 28 percent said "more liberal." A poll released in January 1939 inquired whether voters thought government was spending too much, too little, or about right; 61 percent said too much, 10 percent said too little, and 29 percent said about right.[15]

As Gallup discovered, as the reaction to Roosevelt's Court-packing plan indicated, as the president's approach to Social Security acknowledged, and as various other manifestations of the popular mood of the 1930s suggested, Americans remained skeptical of big government even after a decade of depression. Most were willing to accept a certain expansion of government as a response to the economic emergency. Tighter regulation of the banking and securities industries would help prevent a repetition of the recent fiascoes; relief programs could keep families afloat when no other life preservers were available. But the regulations were basically an extension of the state's police power, and most of the relief programs were perceived as temporary — as they in fact proved to be. Where the Roosevelt administration initiated a positive program intended to be permanent — Social Security, to cite the best example — the designers devised protective coloration that made it look as much like a private program as possible.

By 1940 liberals of sundry shades had been trying for half a century to convince Americans of the merits of more-active government. First the Populists, then the progressives, and finally the New Dealers had preached the necessity of extending Washington's writ. The Populists got almost nothing of what they wanted; the progressives somewhat more; the New Dealers more still. But by most evidence Americans as a group remained unconvinced. Although no one thought it possible to recreate the salutary neglect of the colonial era when government had been three thousand stormy ocean miles away, the belief that government was best kept small and at least at arm's length held firm in the American imagination.

BENEATH THE EAGLE'S WINGS

There was one conspicuous exception to the rule of skepticism of strong government. Since the country's birth as a nation, Americans had looked to government to protect them from armed enemies. In the name of national defense—most conspicuously during wartime—Americans accepted an expansion of government authority that they tolerated under no other circumstances. America's first war spawned its first national government; the country's greatest war of the nineteenth century confirmed the preeminence of the federal government over the states; both world wars of the twentieth century touched off veritable explosions of government into what had been the private sector.

HANGING TOGETHER LEST THEY HANG SEPARATELY

At the time fighting broke out in the American Revolution there existed neither state governments nor a national government. The states themselves were still colonies, and the only thing that even approached a national government was the Continental Congress, which had no authority that bound anyone to anything.

Although the Declaration of Independence of July 1776 converted the colonies into states, it was unclear what, if anything, it converted the Continental Congress into. The states quickly set about writing constitutions and fashioning themselves into practicing polities; the Continental Congress remained essentially a coordinating body, with such slight authority as it possessed deriving entirely from the states.

Yet wars have agendas of their own, and the coordinating the Continental Congress did in the service of independence established certain de facto powers for an American national government. Although the states refused to relinquish their exclusive right to levy taxes — with the cries of "no taxation without representation" still echoing across the land, the taxing power was the most jealously guarded — somebody had to pay for the bread, boots, and bullets that kept George Washington's army in the field. The Continental Congress adopted the expedient of issuing bills of credit, to be redeemed, presumably, when the states came through with their respective contributions. Without explicit authorization to do so the Congress assumed the powers of a national treasury. (The weakness of this scheme, by which Congress could print money but not enforce its redemption, soon gave rise to the phrase "not worth a Continental.") And of course the very conduct of the war made the Congress the equivalent of a war department. A similar ad hoc arrangement gave the Congress the power to conduct a national foreign policy. The first act of American foreign policy was the Declaration of Independence (yet despite its adoption by the Continental Congress, seven of the states felt required to ratify it separately). The second critical undertaking was the negotiation of a treaty of alliance with France, which afforded the initial real hope that the Declaration would have lasting significance.

As a result of the demands of the war the Continental Congress grew from a debating club into the government of an independent nation. In a period when constitution-making obsessed the several states, the desirability of placing the de facto powers of this national government on a legitimate constitutional basis seemed evident to most Americans. Not to all: some states'-rights radicals thought the Congress ought to dissolve itself as soon as the war was over and let the members go home where they belonged. Yet sufficient sentiment supported a continuing national government that the Congress in November 1777 — shortly after the American victory at Saratoga indicated the likelihood of a continuing nation — accepted a constitution, the Articles of Confederation, and sent it on to the states for ratification.

After much wrangling and delay the states accepted the Articles, not least because the powers the national government would exercise under the new constitution were those the Congress had already been exercising under the exigencies of the war. The Confederation government, consisting of a single branch (the Congress), would make war and peace, conduct foreign relations, coin money, adjudicate disputes between states, and handle various lesser tasks. Time — and not much of that — would indicate that other powers ought to be added to the list, but considering the minuscule expectations most Americans had had of national government just a few years earlier, this was no mean accomplishment.

IN UNION, STRENGTH

If the Revolutionary War created a national government, the Civil War preserved it — and in the process expanded federal power further than most people had dreamed before the internecine conflict erupted.

Several of the same issues that had vexed the Continental Congress during the earlier war plagued the administration of Abraham Lincoln after the shooting started at Fort Sumter. Money problems surfaced almost at once and reached critical proportions before the war was a year old. "Immediate action is necessary," Treasury Secretary Salmon Chase warned Congress in February 1862. "The Treasury is nearly empty." Congress responded with three measures that revolutionized the nation's financial structure — at least temporarily. The Legal Tender Act of 1862 created a national currency; but more than that, it made that currency legal tender, which was to say that creditors in nearly all cases were required to accept the greenbacks as payment for debts. Opponents decried the measure as unconstitutional, arguing that when the Constitution granted Congress the power to coin money it meant *coin* money, not paper money. Others screamed breach of contract; to require creditors to accept fiat paper robbed them of their right to real money. Even some supporters acknowledged the strength of the objections — but concluded that the present emergency justified them. "These are extraordinary times," explained Congressman Elbridge Spaulding of New York, "and extraordinary measures must be resorted to in order to save our Government and preserve our nationality."[1]

The currency act paved the way for the National Banking Act of 1863. This measure went far toward reconstructing the federal bank-

ing system Andrew Jackson had destroyed in the 1830s; it authorized the federal charter of banks that would issue banknotes backed
by federal bonds. For two years the construction of this federal
system stalled upon state banks' unwillingness to conform to the
standards required for receipt of the federal charters, but Congress
slapped a tax on state banknotes in 1865, effectively forcing widespread conversion to the federal scheme.

Fully as portentous as the currency and banking acts, and equally
intrusive, was the Internal Revenue Act of 1862. Had Sam Adams
and the Stamp Act rebels of 1765 still lived, they would have de-
spaired at what their efforts on behalf of liberty had led to. The
1862 tax measure levied all manner of charges on alcohol, tobacco,
playing cards, billiard tables, jewelry, yachts, medicines, newspaper
advertisements, professional licenses, business receipts, dividends,
inheritances—and stamps. At the same time it incorporated into
this sweeping system a stopgap measure of August 1861 taxing incomes: the first federal income tax in American history. To collect
the taxes Congress created a Bureau of Internal Revenue (the ante-
cedent of the Internal Revenue Service) and mandated withholding
from corporate dividends and the wages of government employees.

Federal power expanded in other areas related to the war. Federal
funding for a transcontinental railroad served the short-term purpose of spiking pro-Southern sentiment in California, the medium-
term purpose of facilitating troop movements to and from the frontier, and the long-term purpose (assuming the war lasted until the
railroad was completed) of ensuring that California gold and Ne-
vada silver flow freely east, unmolested by the Confederate raiders
that prowled the ocean routes from San Francisco.

More dramatic was the draft. After the trials of battle began to outstrip the voluntarism that had supplied the first several hundred thousand recruits to the Union army, Congress resorted to conscription. This first national draft triggered considerable resentment, not least because a prospective draftee with money could hire a substitute or pay a commutation fee of three hundred dollars and thereby shift the burden to someone else. "In the vast new army of 300,000 which Mr. Lincoln has ordered to be raised," remarked one editor, "there will be not be *one* man able to pay $300. Not one! Think of that!" The resentment erupted most spectacularly — and frighteningly — in New York City during the summer of 1863 when Irish immigrants and others took up arms against the draft, leading to the deaths of more than a hundred people and the destruction of many millions of dollars of property in the worst outbreak of urban violence in American history to that date.[2]

The financial, tax, railroad, and draft measures were the work of Congress; other enlargements of federal power emanated from the White House. Lincoln, worried that Confederate sympathizers would sabotage the Union war effort, repeatedly suspended habeas corpus in suspect areas. When a federal circuit court — presided over, to Lincoln's immediate discomfiture but ultimate advantage, by the notorious defender of slavery, Roger Taney — denied the president's authority to suspend this crucial civil liberty, Lincoln pleaded necessity in ignoring the court's decree. "Are all the laws, *but one* [habeas corpus], to go unexecuted," Lincoln asked rhetorically, "and the government itself go to pieces, lest that one be violated?" In other cases — including a prosecution of Ohio gubernatorial candidate and Copperhead Clement Vallandigham — the president tacitly approved the use of military courts in neighborhoods far from the fighting, in order to silence critics of administration policy.[3]

Lincoln's disregard for constitutional rights and legal procedure provoked outrage even among those who sympathized with his cause; abolitionist Wendell Phillips branded the president "a more unlimited despot than the world knows this side of China." But in certain respects the most breathtaking expansion of federal power during the Civil War was Lincoln's Emancipation Proclamation. With a stroke of his pen the president sliced through decades of debate regarding the authority of the federal government to regulate or otherwise constrain the "peculiar institution." With the same stroke he wiped out billions of dollars of what passed for private property in the Confederacy. Lincoln himself had reservations about his prerogatives in this regard, which was one reason the proclamation initially pertained only to those areas in rebellion against the Union, where his war powers most patently applied. Yet anyone — in the South, in the North, in the border states — could see that the announcement of September 22, 1862, changed everything about the slavery question. If the North won the war — as, after Antietam, appeared increasingly likely — slavery would vanish from the country that in 1861 was the world's foremost slave power.[4]

Lincoln's nervousness on emancipation led him to insist that it be written into the Constitution as soon as possible. The Thirteenth Amendment, though not enacted until shortly after the war (and after Lincoln's death), was to all intents and purposes a wartime measure. So, albeit at slightly farther remove, were the Fourteenth and Fifteenth Amendments. The Thirteenth and Fifteenth Amendments were relatively narrow in scope, but the Fourteenth Amendment — in particular its "due process" clause — eventually provided the basis for almost revolutionary extensions of federal power, as by the "incorporation" of the Bill of Rights against the states.

(Significantly for the purpose of the present argument, the major part of the incorporation took place under the Warren Supreme Court of the 1960s.)

MR. WILSON'S WAR

Like all American presidents, Woodrow Wilson was initially elected for his views on domestic issues, and for the first year-and-a-half of his tenure he devoted himself to converting his New Freedom philosophy into practice. In August 1914, however, the outbreak of war in Europe rudely reminded Americans of the world beyond the sea. During the next thirty-two months the war gradually pulled the United States closer and closer, until Wilson asked for and got a war declaration in April 1917.

Many, likely most, members of Congress — even among those who voted for war — had no real idea what modern warfare entailed. The Spanish-American War of 1898 had been splendidly small and short, amounting to little more than a summer fling with soldiering. The Civil War resided in the living memory of only the oldest citizens, whose number and influence — and memories — decreased with each anniversary of Appomattox. And in any event, the Civil War meant nothing personal to those tens of millions of immigrants who had been flooding the nation's ports of entry since the 1880s.

To be sure, Americans of 1917 had read of the carnage at the Somme and seen photographs of the terrible trenches. And what they had read and seen convinced them — again including even many of those who voted for war — that the United States should stay out of the mud of northern France. Submarine attacks on American shipping were the immediate casus belli; sinking German submarines didn't require infantry divisions and barbed wire. That was what navies were for. Within the week of the American declaration of war, an aide to War Secretary Newton Baker briefed the Senate finance committee on a $3 billion emergency appropriation the war department was requesting to meet the suddenly changed circumstances.

"Three billions!" answered the shocked committee chairman, Thomas Martin. "What do you want it for?"

Clothing, food, medical supplies, horses, mules, airplanes, balloons, and a thousand other things, explained the aide. Sending soldiers to France would be expensive.

"Good Lord!" spluttered Martin. "You're not going to send soldiers over there, are you?" After he recovered his composure, Martin amended his question to a declaration: "Congress will not permit American soldiers to be sent to Europe."[5]

But indeed Congress did—and not only did it *permit* American soldiers to be sent to Europe but it ordered them overseas. In contrast to the Civil War, when the government had turned to conscription belatedly (and provoked such hostility), the Wilson administration sought a draft from the start. Administration spokesmen trotted out various rationales for this renewed intrusion on citizens' lives. A draft, as opposed to reliance on volunteers, would ensure that the nation's war for democracy be fought by a democratic army—or at least one drawn from all classes and stations. "Universal training," said George Creel, the administration's chief propagandist, employing the euphemism of choice for mandatory enlistment, "will jumble the boys of America all together, shoulder to shoulder, smashing all the petty class distinctions that now divide, and prompting a brand of real democracy." (The irrepressible Creel went on to predict additionally that universal service would regenerate "the heart, liver, and kidneys of America," which were "in sad need of overhauling.")

Wilson himself justified the draft by denying that it signified any serious coercion at all. "It is in no sense a conscription of the unwilling," the president explained; it was merely a procedure for "selection from a nation which has volunteered in mass."[6]

Such sophistry hardly persuaded everyone. Amos Pinchot, one of Theodore Roosevelt's strongest supporters against Wilson in 1912, damned the draft as a capitalist plot to intimidate American workers. Pinchot castigated as "pure, unadulterated bunk" the argument of Creel and the conscriptionists that mandatory service was necessary to American defense; far from defending democracy, a draft would destroy it. "In this country so ordered and so governed there will be no more strikes, no surly revolt against authority and no popular discontent. In it the lamb will lie down with the lion, and he will lie down right where the lion tells him to. In it there will be government for the people, plenty of it, extending into every detail of life; but there will be mighty little government of or by the people." Speaker of the House Champ Clark of Missouri dryly declared: "In the estimation of Missourians there is precious little difference between a conscript and a convict."[7]

Wilson nevertheless insisted on his draft (in some indeterminable part because reliance on volunteers might have forced him to accept Roosevelt's offer to raise new Rough Riders — the mere thought of which the president couldn't abide). And despite the widespread distrust he got it.

Conscription was only the start. On the same reasoning that dictated the drafting of workers into the national service, the Wilson administration drafted management as well — albeit on considerably better terms than the workers received. During the summer of 1917 Wilson unveiled something called the War Industries Board. Initially designed to coordinate the administration's war purchases, the board's appetite grew with the eating. It became downright rav-enous upon takeover by Bernard Baruch, one of the sharpest minds in American finance. Baruch brought some baggage to his job; Wilson confidant Edward House worried that the country might not take kindly to "a Hebrew Wall Street speculator given so much power." Yet Baruch had compensating gifts, including what one associate called his willingness to "look any man in the eye and tell him to go to hell."[8]

Whether because of Baruch's religion, his occupation, his blunt-ness, or his power, many Americans *did* object to the work of the war board. In the interest of production speed, if not necessarily efficiency, the board encouraged cooperation among former indus-trial rivals. It suspended price competition in large areas of govern-ment purchasing, instead apportioning purchase orders by decree. Such centralization would have stuck in the craw of many of the participating businessmen had they not been so busy pocketing the profits from the war-induced boom.

To Wilson critics like Champ Clark this cartelizing arrangement appeared entirely too cozy—an irresistible temptation to price-fixing. "The Attorney General should put every one of those fellows in jail between now and Saturday night who keep the price up," the Democratic lawmaker said at a moment of special exasperation with a group of raw-materials producers. But the centralizing went re-lentlessly forward, swept on by the general enthusiasm for the war.[9]

Lest the enthusiasm flag, the administration launched unexam-pled initiatives in the field of public relations. Wartime governments have always sought to rally the masses against the foe du jour; to Wilson's generation of progressives, convinced that education, properly conceived and directed, held the solution to most social evils, propaganda came especially naturally. Indeed, some of the first

federal forays into propaganda took the form of educational programs for the nation's secondary schools and colleges. These "war
study courses" were designed to ensure that students understand
what their government was about to send them—the males, anyway—off to France to die for.

Indoctrination assumed other forms as well. George Creel's
Committee on Public Information organized all manner of activities
aimed to educate and motivate Americans regarding the guilt of
Germany and the need for America to deliver chastisement. Creel
recruited from the ranks of investigative journalism, that seedbed of
progressivism, drawing in such muckraking stalwarts as Ray Stannard Baker and Ida Tarbell. He also enlisted tens of thousands of
"four-minute men" who in their 240 seconds of fame in front of
movie-theater and other audiences preached Prussian atrocity, Al-
lied steadfastness, and American heroism. By Creel's own reckoning
the four-minute program had the "sweep of a prairie fire" and "the
projectile force of a French '75.'" Before long the snappy speeches
were being supplemented by equally punchy sessions of song, the
aim of which, according to the directive from Creel's office, was to
maintain home-front patriotism at "white heat."[10]

When the fast-talkers got down to specifics, they frequently
flogged Liberty bonds. These were intended to ease the burden of
financing the war, and to a substantial degree they did. But they
never carried the war's whole fiscal weight—most of the rest of
which was held up by federal taxes. As in the case of propaganda, so
in tax policy did the requirements of war dovetail with the inclina-
tions of the progressives. When Congress and the states had debated
the Sixteenth Amendment in the years before its 1913 adoption,
next to none of the proponents of a national income tax had antici-

pated that its first serious test would be a world war. Yet the fortuitous availability of an income tax allowed the Wilson administration and Congress to consider funding the war effort to a historically unprecedented degree from current tax revenues rather than by borrowing. This decision reflected both an acknowledged and widely commended desire to avoid lading future generations with a large debt, and a less-often-cited desire to use the war to leverage a permanent shift in the source of federal revenues from regressive excise taxes and tariffs to progressive (in both senses) personal and corporate income taxes.

Predictably, those who stood to bear the tax increases protested. Business lobbyists complained that so-called excess-profits taxes unfairly targeted essential war industries and penalized efficiency besides. Moreover, recognizing what the progressives were up to, they objected that the middle of a war was hardly the time to make fundamental changes in the philosophy of federal finance.

Progressives in turn derided the objections. "Our endeavors to impose heavy war profit taxes," observed Theodore Roosevelt's former partner on the 1912 Bull Moose ticket, Hiram Johnson, "have brought into sharp relief the skin-deep dollar patriotism of some of those who have been loudest in declamations on war and in their demands for blood."[11]

The tax resisters beat back some of the increases but by no means all. The war years witnessed a revolution in American tax policy. Before the war the federal tax code was mildly to sharply regressive, relying heavily on customs duties and excise taxes, which together constituted more than 70 percent of the total federal take; after the war it was far more progressive, with the bulk of revenues deriving from personal and corporate income taxes and estate taxes (customs and excise taxes had fallen to less than 20 percent of the total). Corporate income taxes nearly quadrupled between 1916 and 1920, from $172 million to $637 million, while personal income taxes, the levy most noticed by individuals, more than quintupled, from $173 million to more than $1 billion. The wealthiest individuals encountered the largest increase, with the tax rate on incomes of $1 million soaring from 10 percent in 1916 to 66 percent in 1920. And there was simply a great deal more of taxes total. The federal government took in $761 million in 1916 and $6.6 billion in 1920. (Yet even with this eight-fold increase in revenues, Washington fell considerably shy of paying for the war out of pocket. The federal debt skyrocketed from $1.2 billion in 1916 to more than $24 billion in 1920.)[12]

One measure of government intrusiveness is the size of the bite government takes out of people's incomes; another is the sensitivity of government's hearing, especially of dissenting opinions. During World War I the Wilson administration showed itself to be fully as sensitive to dissent as the Lincoln administration had been during the Civil War. Updated espionage and sedition acts gave the government cover for attempting to suppress most forms of written and spoken opposition. Postmaster General Albert Sidney Burleson barred troublesome papers and magazines from the mails; journalists could criticize, he explained, but added significantly: "There is a limit." That limit was reached when a paper "begins to say that this Government got in the war wrong, that it is in it for the wrong purposes, or anything that will impugn the motives of the Government for going into the war. They can not say that this Government is the tool of Wall Street or the munitions-makers. . . . There can be no campaign against conscription and the Draft Law." Burleson's fellow Texan, Attorney General Thomas Gregory, was even more explicit. Speaking of critics of the administration's war policies, Gregory declared: "May God have mercy on them, for they need expect none from an outraged people and an avenging government."[13]

Between them, Burleson and Gregory went far toward suppressing opinions not in tune with the administration's war policies. Famous critics like Theodore Roosevelt could get away with attacking the government, although even Roosevelt suspected that Burleson's boys were opening his mail. Beyond his stature as an ex-president, it probably benefited Roosevelt that he advocated *harsher* war policies rather than weaker. Critics with less distinguished resumés or who advanced opinions casting doubt on the entire enterprise of the war came in for rougher treatment. Gregory's avengers nailed socialist Eugene Debs for speaking against the war; Debs went to prison for the duration (and then some—he was still behind bars in November 1920 when he received nearly one million votes for president).

The G-men weren't sufficiently numerous, however, to snuff out the disloyalty Burleson and Gregory saw everywhere, so the administration reinforced them with semi-official watchdogs of the quasi-governmental American Protective League. By 1918 there were a quarter-million of these card-carrying, badge-bearing special agents peering into their neighbors' windows, eavesdropping on conversations, pawing through garbage, and otherwise making many times their number nervous. The APL agents participated in "slacker raids" against suspected draft dodgers; the largest raid, in September 1918, collared more than fifty thousand in the New York City area alone. Even though two-thirds of those taken into custody were discovered to have committed no violation, the Justice Department was pleased. Assistant Attorney General John Lord O'Brian observed — accurately enough — that America had never been more thoroughly policed.[14]

THE ARSENAL OF DEMOCRACY

In certain respects World War II was just like World War I, only bigger. This was true of the death and destruction the second war wreaked across the globe; it was also true of the centralizing tendencies it triggered in the United States. Nearly every federal agency or office established in 1917 or 1918 to facilitate the war effort had its counterpart in the early 1940s; these counterparts were usually bigger, as befit the larger conflict, and there were more of them. George Creel's Committee on Public Information became the Office of War Information; Bernard Baruch's War Industries Board was transmogrified into the War Production Board, which was assisted by the Office of War Mobilization. There were also a War Labor Board, a War Manpower Commission, a War Shipping Administration, an Office of Defense Transportation, an Office of Price Administration, an Office of Scientific Research and Development, and lesser offices and agencies too numerous to mention.

Changing times necessitated changing techniques. Where the war-study courses of the earlier conflict had been traditional books-and-lectures affairs, their counterparts the second time around were supplemented by instructional and motivational films produced by the education division of the Office of War Information. The four-minute men gave way to propaganda films shown before Hollywood's features (themselves strongly influenced by the war effort). Radio afforded a new mass medium for getting the patriotic message out; the OWI's radio bureau lauded not only America's own virtues but those of America's allies ("Soviet Union hits the spot / Twelve million soldiers that's a lot / Timoshenko and Stalin too / Soviet Union is Red, White and Blue").[15]

At times the war effort seemed chiefly an exercise in marketing. The Office of Civilian Defense promoted the concept of the V-Home, the patriotic household that assiduously supported the men on the fighting front — perhaps including Daddy — by conserving essential goods, salvaging materials that could be recycled, purchasing war stamps and bonds, and refusing to spread rumors that might divide or dispirit the nation. Ad agencies that had spent the previous generation persuading Americans to buy more of everything were now employed to convince the country that less was more ("Use it up / Wear it out / Make it do / Or do without").[16]

In small part because of sour memories from the first war, and in larger part because there was almost no antiwar sentiment this time around, the civil liberties of most Americans fared better than before. Even the hard-to-please American Civil Liberties Union thought so, discerning a "heartening contrast" between world wars on this subject.[17]

There was one glaring exception, however: the roundup, relocation, and effective imprisonment of Japanese-Americans in the western states. Before the war almost no one would have thought Franklin Roosevelt capable of such heavy-handed treatment of such a large segment (comprising more than a hundred thousand persons) of the American population. Not even Abraham Lincoln, on a great deal more evidence of disloyalty among the Copperheads, had swung the stick of raw power with such abandon. That the Supreme Court subsequently upheld the president's action confirmed both that Oliver Wendell Holmes, Jr., wasn't Roger Taney and that Americans had become inured to the most sweeping measures undertaken in the name of national security.

For Americans not of Japanese descent, the most obvious manifestation of wartime federal authority was the mobilization of the economy. Again the model was World War I; again the scope was much greater. As Donald Nelson of the War Production Board explained, his agency, compared to its counterpart of the earlier conflict, "was ten times as large, just as our war needs were ten times as large." And just as the emergency of war in 1917 had allowed certain tendencies of the progressives to blossom, so did the crisis of 1942 encourage the centralizing tendencies of the New Dealers. Edwin Witte, one of the drafters of the Social Security Act of 1935, joined the War Labor Board, and from the vantage point of January 1943 assessed recent developments with satisfaction: "Our economy is rapidly becoming a completely planned economy."[18]

And that was after but a year of war. Before the fighting ended, the federal government had a hand, sometimes two, in nearly every aspect of American economic relations. War production, of course, followed the strictest federal guidelines — except regarding antitrust, which was suspended for the duration. Competition largely vanished, in favor of cost-plus pricing on contracts awarded by federal bureaucrats working closely with "dollar-a-year" men on loan from private industry. Federal regulators fixed prices for all kinds of goods, set ceilings for production of consumer items, and issued ration coupons dictating who got how many of what. Whole industries, including those producing automobiles and consumer appliances, were shut down, with the manufacturers essentially compelled to retool for war production.

Washington's reach extended into the most unlikely arenas. After the Japanese captured the Southeast Asian sources of the largest part of the world's rubber, the federal government decreed that women's girdles were superfluous to the war effort and therefore not deserving of manufacture. (This fit nicely with other decrees declaring delicacies high in fat and sugar to be unpatriotically indulgent when consumed in more than the smallest quantities. *McCall's* fashion forecaster commented: "Just what the lack of girdles will do to fashion is anybody's guess, but Washington's experts don't hold out much hope for a return to solid, hefty bulges. Stay slim for healthy beauty and morale — that's their advice.") On the other hand, the War Production Board ruled in favor of face powder, lipstick, and rouge, declaring that not only did a girl get a lift from a visit to the beauty shop, but "her resultant vivacious spirit, self-confidence and geniality, being infectious, are transmuted directly to the male members of the family."[19]

Other enlargements of federal authority were equally prosaic but no less portentous. On the premise that workers had to sleep somewhere, Roosevelt decreed the disbursement of federal funds for the construction of housing. In Detroit, where the factories that lately had churned out cars now poured forth planes and tanks, the U.S. Housing Authority directed the building of the Sojourner Truth housing project, a complex of 1,000 units. (Twenty percent of these were set aside for African American families — a point that angered many white residents of the city, with results that included one of the worst race riots in American history and thereby cast a long shadow over this early foray into federally financed housing.)

The children of workers had special needs. As the nation's industrial war machine geared up, workers went where the jobs were, taking their children and often overwhelming school districts in the job-rich regions. Until this time local financing of schools had been an article of the American civic religion; now, under the duress of war, the local districts pleaded for help. On the reasoning that the national emergency was causing the local crises, Washington answered the pleas. The initial appropriation, in 1941, amounted to $150 million, with payments keyed to the local costs per pupil; the program subsequently grew, quietly but steadily.[20]

Another pathbreaking foray carried the federal government to the frontier of scientific and technological research. An immediate impetus to the expedition was a later-famous (but at the time top-secret) letter from Albert Einstein to Roosevelt explaining that the Germans were almost certainly trying to harness the newly discovered power of the atom for military purposes; the United States must move quickly to preempt Hitler's scientists. A deeper cause for government involvement in science was retrospective embarrassment at the failure of the Allies during World War I to effectively marshal their scientific resources — or even their scientists, many of whom were funneled into the trenches along with the rest of the cannon fodder. (The Germans had done much better, albeit not well enough to win the war.) From this mix of reasons, the federal government quickly set about inventorying the country's scientific talent and putting it to optimal use. Much of the work sponsored by the Office of Scientific Research and Development was kept out of sight; the biggest of the clandestine programs was the Manhattan atom bomb project. But the Manhattan men (and the few women) spent only a small portion of Washington's research-and-development money; by the end of the war the federal government was far and away the largest sponsor and consumer of scientific and technical knowledge in the country — as by then it was the largest sponsor and consumer of nearly everything else produced in the country. In 1945 the federal government spent ten times as much as it had in 1939; in the last year of the war, government spending constituted nearly half the gross national product.[21]

World War II confirmed a pattern of anomaly in American history. Against a background of persistent distrust of government's growth, Americans accepted the expansion — sometimes the breathtaking expansion — of federal authority during wartime. As much as they looked to the private sector for their prosperity and happiness during the long stretches of peace, they looked to government for their defense during periods of war. And they defined in increasingly generous fashion what the national defense entailed.

3 THE WAR THAT NEVER ENDED

Historically, what had made each wartime expansion of government tolerable was the general understanding that it was temporary. After the Revolutionary War, after the Civil War, and after World War I, Americans lost little time reversing the growth of government those conflicts had engendered.

The 1781 victory at Yorktown, and even more so Britain's formal acknowledgment of American independence at Paris two years later, removed the external stimulus to cooperation that had persuaded the states to make common cause during the war. Militia drafts were terminated, leaving soldiers to go back to their farms and forges; requisitions by the Congress upon the states became even harder to collect; the states began conducting their own commercial policies — frequently against one another. Compared with the powers of the governments of other countries, the powers of the American national government since 1776 had never been great, but at the end of the war such spirit of patriotic cooperation as had at least intermittently inspired the separate states to pull together largely vanished. Historians no longer look on the "critical period" of the 1780s as being quite so dire as it once seemed — most now would place the patient on the serious but stable list — but the situation appeared to contemporaries to be sufficiently threatening that they shortly decided to reverse some of the reversal and strengthen the central government via a new constitution — albeit one circumscribed closely by a bill of rights.

The ebb of federal power after the Civil War was complicated by the requirements of Reconstruction. Within the Northern states most of the overburden of wartime governance — including conscription, detention without trial, and suppression of dissent — was lifted more or less at once. Other wartime measures survived a little longer: the federal income tax didn't disappear until 1872. But in the states of the defeated South the apparatus of war remained in place until those states were reintegrated into the Union, at times that varied from state to state and didn't end completely until a dozen years after Appomattox. Yet when it finally *was* removed, the South was arguably freer of Washington's influence than the North. For predictable reasons the lifting of federal military rule produced a backlash against federal authority. Not even the Constitution, newly amended, stood proof against the rejection of Washington and nearly all its works. During the next quarter-century white majorities in the South largely succeeded — by poll taxes, literacy tests, and less subtle forms of intimidation — in nullifying the Fifteenth Amendment as it applied to African-Americans; and by analogous official and unofficial methods they made serious inroads on the Thirteenth and Fourteenth Amendments. At the same time, the return of Southern Democrats to federal politics slammed shut the window of opportunity that had allowed such Republican projects as the Homestead and Morrill Acts to slip through.

After World War I the retreat of federal power occurred more quickly and uniformly. The War Industries Board, the Office of War Information, and the other agencies created to coordinate the war effort went out of business shortly after imperial Germany did. Certain wartime measures remained on the books for a matter of months or a few years: Attorney General A. Mitchell Palmer took advantage of the still-operative Alien Act (a companion to the Sedition Act) in late 1919 and the first half of 1920 to round up and deport hundreds of allegedly subversive non-citizens (a category construed to comprise many labor activists as well as true-red Bolsheviks). On the whole, however, the Republicans who gained control of Congress in the 1918 elections and the White House in 1920 were happy to loosen the hold Washington had acquired on the economy during the war, and they and nearly everyone else were happy to loosen the hold Washington had acquired on so much else. The throat-tightening exception to this general trend was Prohibition — which proved either that there are exceptions to every rule or that the exceptions to the exceptions, in this case the effective nullification of the Volstead Act in many cities, can be more indicative of popular sentiment than the exceptions themselves.

At the end of World War II, nearly all Americans anticipated another instance of the historic pattern of the postwar retreat of federal authority. Events briefly fulfilled their expectations. But before long, something new in their experience surfaced to halt the retreat, then reverse it. Americans discovered to their dismay that they were still at war, and they readjusted their thinking accordingly.

DEMOBILIZATION DERAILED

On V-J Day in August 1945, the first order of business for those who had borne the weight of the world war and for their dependents, fiancées, relatives, and friends was the return of the GIs to ordinary life. Few civilians — or soldiers either, for that matter — had any real appreciation of the logistical immensities of retrieving 10 million men from the far corners of the earth and mustering them out in a more or less orderly fashion, and when Johnny didn't come marching home quickly, complaints rained down on Washington. Babies, with maternal assistance on addresses and postage, mailed their booties to senators and representatives, demanding their daddies' return from Europe and the Pacific. The daddies weighed in with riots in camps in Germany.

The besieged legislators set for themselves a de facto deadline of November 1946 for restoring their heroes — that is, their constituents — to family life; meanwhile they commenced dismantling the enormous federal superstructure that had developed during the war. Agencies, offices, and commissions were terminated by the dozens; bureaucrats were released by the thousands; contracts were canceled by the millions of dollars. Censorship, both formal and tacit, essentially ceased; surveillance of suspect individuals drastically diminished upon the disappearance of the wartime grounds for such suspicion.

But the demobilization hadn't come anywhere near completion before doubts began to surface that a return to the kind of normality that had followed previous wars was desirable or even possible. The attempted isolation of the 1930s was generally perceived, with post-Munich, post-Pearl Harbor hindsight, to have been doomed from the start; now nearly everyone in the United States accepted the notion of a larger continuing role for their country in world politics. The nature of this role remained open to energetic debate. Many Americans looked to the nascent United Nations to keep the peace. These internationalists anticipated that the United States would take an active part in U.N. activities — in contrast to America's boycott of the League of Nations — but that this part wouldn't necessarily be much more than that of first among equals. Others expected a spheres-of-influence approach to the peace, with the United States essentially policing a portion of the globe much as it had policed the Western Hemisphere for half a century.

The big question mark in all such calculations was the Kremlin. Would the Soviets remain the grand allies they had been during the fight against Hitler? Or would they revert to the revolutionary Bolshevism of the early days of the Soviet Union? If the former turned out to be the case, then America's postwar role, either within the United Nations or as a gendarme of some slice of the planet, might be relatively modest. If Stalin took up the cudgels of revolution, however, the United States might find it necessary to do rather more.

Events of the eighteen months after the war suggested — to the Truman administration at least — that Stalin was indeed intent on spreading revolution. Red Army troops remained in occupation of nearly all the territory they had liberated from the Germans, and under that occupation local Communists steadily shoved aside competing parties. Poland appeared to be the test case of the Kremlin's designs: there Stalin was openly flouting the — admittedly loosely drafted — Yalta accord that committed him to allow participation in government by non-Communist groups. Because the war had started in 1939 over the violation of Poland's independence, this postwar violation appeared particularly provocative. Other indications of uncooperativeness — the Red Army's looting of Moscow's zone of Germany, its tardiness in evacuating Iran, a speech by Stalin declaring the fundamental incompatibility of capitalism and socialism — aggravated American suspicions.

These suspicions began to achieve critical mass during the first half of 1946. In a long and subsequently famous telegram home from Moscow, diplomat George Kennan warned, "We have here a political force committed fanatically to the belief that with [the] U.S. there can be no permanent modus vivendi, that it is desirable and necessary that the internal harmony of our society be disrupted, our traditional way of life be destroyed, the international authority of our state be broken, if Soviet power is to be secure."[1]

Kennan's alarum echoed down the corridors of the State Department and the Pentagon, and it afforded support to the growing group who believed that the United States mustn't lower the guard it had built up at such expense during the late war. Although maintaining wartime levels of manpower was utterly out of the question, maintaining — or augmenting — American firepower was not. The War and Navy Departments (soon to be married in the Defense Department) quietly continued development of advanced weapons, including atomic bombs and intercontinental bombers. (Certain aspects of the development — such as above-ground atomic tests — weren't so quiet.) These departments and the State Department arranged agreements by which the United States acquired rights to several score of air and naval bases around the world. And despite the mustering out of many millions of American servicemen, U.S. occupation troops in Germany, Japan, and Korea showed no sign of imminent evacuation.

RECALL TO ARMS

Many Americans didn't realize the extent of their government's change of heart until Truman delivered a momentous address to Congress in March 1947. The address followed confidential news from London that the British could no longer afford to stabilize the status quo in Greece and Turkey, as they had for years. Truman might have responded with a narrow affirmation of American support for the Greek government, then confronting a Communist insurgency, and the Turkish government, under diplomatic pressure from the Soviet Union. Some of his advisers recommended he adopt precisely such a cautious course. But he ignored their advice, believing that American security required putting the matter as starkly as possible. He returned an early draft to his speechwriters, complaining that it sounded "like an investment prospectus." He demanded something much tougher. "We had fought a long and costly war to crush the totalitarianism of Hitler, the insolence of Mussolini, and the arrogance of the warlords of Japan," he explained afterward. "Yet the new menace facing us seemed every bit as grave as Nazi Germany and her allies had been. . . . I wanted no hedging in this speech. This was America's answer to the surge of expansion of Communist tyranny. It had to be clear and free of hesitation or double talk."[2]

Truman's speech was all of that. "At the present moment in world history," he told a joint session of Congress on March 12, "nearly every nation must choose between alternative ways of life. . . . One way of life is based upon the will of the majority, and is distinguished by free institutions, representative government, free elections, guarantees of individual liberty, freedom of speech and religion, and freedom from political oppression. The second way of life is based upon the will of a minority forcibly imposed upon the majority. It relies upon terror and oppression, a controlled press and radio, fixed elections, and the suppression of personal freedom." The president proceeded to enunciate what quickly became known as the Truman doctrine: "I believe that it must be the policy of the United States to support free peoples who are resisting attempted subjugation by armed minorities or by outside pressures." He hoped at this point that such support might remain chiefly economic. But he offered no guarantee that it would, and when he compared the $400 million he was currently requesting to the $341 *billion* America had spent during the recent world war, listeners might have been forgiven for guessing that the water they were being invited into was deeper than it looked.[3]

And so it was. Truman's request for $400 million for Greece and Turkey turned out to be a small down payment on what the administration shortly revealed to be an ambitious effort to stem the advance of communism. In June 1947 Secretary of State George Marshall unveiled a plan — or rather the outline of a plan — under which the United States would underwrite the reconstruction of the economies of Western Europe. A belief that prosperity was the surest safeguard against communism motivated the Marshall plan, as did a conviction that economic integration was the most reliable safeguard against another war like the last two. This second judgment caused American officials to require the Europeans to begin coordinating their economies as a condition of aid. Those countries under Soviet control were issued pro forma invitations, but because Moscow refused to allow the required moves toward integration with the West, the invitations came to naught — eliciting relief from administration officials who reckoned they would have a hard enough time selling the package to Congress even without Communist participation.

The Marshall plan did require selling. It would be larger by a factor of twenty or thirty than the aid package to Greece and Turkey, and the Republicans who had recently regained control of Congress — after a decade-and-a-half in the New Deal wilderness — were in no mood to fund profligacy, especially by a still-Democratic

White House. Although most of the Marshall money would be earmarked for the purchase of American-made goods, the very apparatus that ensured that the money be spent where it was supposed to be spent promised to reprise some of the regimented experience of the war years.

And then there was the separate but no less central issue of entanglement in the internal affairs of Europe. According to the administration, the Europeans were to devise the required plan for cooperation, but here again American oversight — if not outright American direction — would be necessary. Where would it lead? Senator Robert Taft thought the whole scheme would simply play into Moscow's hands. "If we throw our dollars around and try to run the show," the Ohio Republican declared, "we are going to give the Communists further arguments against us for trying to be imperialistic."[4]

In the end, however, the same arguments that sold the Greek-Turkish aid plan persuaded the legislature to fund the Marshall plan. Communism was the current face of aggressive totalitarianism; having sacrificed so much to defeat fascism, the United States couldn't afford not to spend this comparatively little more to secure democracy again. The Communists corroborated the administration's arguments by seizing control of Czechoslovakia and blockading Berlin, thereby lending credence to the contention that Stalin was really Hitler in red.

THE GREAT DEBATE BEGINS

Yet pledging American locomotives and cement-mixers to Europe was quite a different matter than pledging American lives, and when the Truman administration began talking of opening an

American military umbrella over the western half of the continent, more than just opposition Republicans objected. The North Atlantic alliance contradicted a century-and-a-half of American tradition and denied the wisdom of George Washington, Thomas Jefferson, John Quincy Adams, Henry Clay, Henry Cabot Lodge, and lesser luminaries. If God had intended for Americans to garrison Europe, He wouldn't have created the Atlantic Ocean.

The rejoinder, of course, was the same one that had led Congress to vote for war in 1917 and again in 1941. Whatever God had intended in digging the Atlantic, the old moat wasn't what it used to be. The general lesson of the twentieth century was that any major war would eventually entangle the United States; the particular lesson of the 1930s was that aggression had to be stopped before it acquired momentum. No one wanted another war, but the way to prevent war was to prepare for it—which was something else George Washington had said. Putting Moscow on notice that any misbehavior would provoke an American reaction was the best method of encouraging good behavior.

George Washington wasn't the only one cited on both sides of the debate over the North Atlantic treaty of 1949. Each side took the arguments of the other and turned them on their heads. Conservatives like Robert Taft linked the proposed expansion of American responsibilities overseas to unnerving trends that ran back more than a decade. "The measures undertaken by the Democratic Administration are alarming," he had declared during Franklin Roosevelt's first term. "Whatever may be said for them as emergency measures, their permanent incorporation into our system would practically abandon the whole theory of American government, and inaugurate what is in fact socialism." Taft mightily resisted American involvement in World War II. Even four months after Pearl Harbor he was able to opine that "we need not have become involved in the present war." Looking back on that war from the perspective of the Cold War, he still held that he had been right. "I don't see how we could be any worse off than we are today."

In Taft's view the Cold War was a direct outgrowth of the big-government, save-the-world philosophy that had produced the New Deal and American involvement in the recent world war. "We have quietly adopted a tendency to interfere in the affairs of other na-tions," he said at the beginning of 1949, "to assume that we are a kind of demigod and Santa Claus to solve the problems of the world." This was a grave mistake, and it ought to be reversed. Taft loudly opposed the North Atlantic treaty. He contended that it was unnec-essary: if the Soviets intended to invade Western Europe, why hadn't they done so in 1946 when that region was prostrate, rather than waiting until now when it was back on its feet? Taft said he wouldn't object to a unilateral declaration to Stalin to mind his own affairs, but this business of ringing Russia with American-armed allies might well provoke the war it was supposed to prevent. Moreover it would foster a kind of defense dependency in Europe that would be deleterious to American interests. The British and other Europeans evidently intended to trade with Moscow; Taft predicted that "the more we take off their shoulders the burden of providing for their own defense, the more free they will be to ship steel and heavy machinery to the east." Americans were paying too much already for what their government told them was necessary for their welfare. "I do not think that the American people at this time desire to increase the overall aid we are giving to western Europe with its tremendous burden on the American taxpayer."

Taft hated what the world war had done by way of expanding the sphere of government, and he dreaded a repetition. "History shows that once power is granted it is impossible for the people to get it back," he had declared during the 1930s. "In Greece republics gave way to tyrannies. The Roman Republic became an empire." Now he saw the same thing happening in the United States under the cover of this military alliance and the other manifestations of the Cold War. "It is easy to slip into an attitude of imperialism where war becomes an instrument of public policy rather than its last resort."[5]

But Taft's was a rearguard and ultimately futile action. "My friend from Ohio," commented Arthur Vandenberg, leader of the Cold War Republicans in the Senate, "has given me a first class headache tonight." Vandenberg added, "I get so damned sick of that little band of GOP isolationists who are always in the way that I could scream." Eighty-one of Vandenberg's Senate colleagues concurred — on the merits of NATO if not on the need for aspirin and scream therapy to counter Taft's arguments — while only a dozen sided with Taft against the treaty.[6]

THE NEW THEOLOGY

In their critique of the Cold War imperium, conservatives like Taft could point to a growing phalanx of the instrumentalities of empire. The first half-decade of the Cold War witnessed the creation of a daunting national security bureaucracy, centered in the National Security Council and comprising the Department of Defense, the Central Intelligence Agency, the State Department's Policy Planning Staff, and assorted other agencies. Hard-core conservative conspiratorialists saw in this growth a grand design; the more perspicacious of those on the right, including Taft, recognized a pattern less deliberate but for that reason all the more insidious. The hunger for power, they contended, whether over domestic affairs or foreign, was never sated. True conservatives had to be as vigilant against the extension of government power overseas as against encroachments at home, for anything that whetted the appetite in one sphere whetted it in the other.

The actions of the new bureaucracies certainly seemed to bear out Taft's warnings — or at least they would have if those actions had been open to public view. Of course this was another source of conservative concern: because agencies like the NSC and the CIA conducted much of their business beyond the view of the public, there was no way of knowing what mischief they were up to.

What they were chiefly up to in the spring of 1950 was an articulation of American policy in the Cold War. In August 1949 the Soviet Union had revealed — to those with Geiger counters downwind — that it had figured out how to construct an atomic bomb. Two months later the Kremlin's co-ideologists in China, led by Mao Zedong, completed the Communist victory there and added China's 600 million people to the legions of Lenin and Marx. All of a sudden the world was looking even more dangerous than it had merely several months before. Truman commissioned his National Security Council to determine just how dangerous it was, and what the United States ought to do to meet the danger.

The answers appeared in a policy paper called NSC-68, although "Anti-Communist Manifesto" would have been more like it. The paper, drafted three years after the Truman doctrine, revealed how thoroughly the national security apparatus had adopted the Manichean mindset of the Cold War. The world was divided into two warring camps, the authors said: the camp of freedom, led by the United States and based on the Declaration of Independence and a belief in the dignity and worth of the individual, and the camp of communism, led by the Soviet Union and based on the principle of dictatorship and world conquest. Put more succinctly: "There is a basic conflict between the idea of freedom under a government of laws, and the idea of slavery under the grim oligarchy of the Kremlin." At one time Americans had thought the affairs of other countries didn't concern them. Such an attitude today would court disaster. "The assault on free institutions is world-wide now, and in the context of the present polarization of power a defeat of free institutions anywhere is a defeat everywhere."

There was more along these lines, including a detailed description of the Communists' multipronged psychological, political, and economic offensive of subversion, manipulation, and intimidation. Soviet industrial performance was assessed in terms of the production of crude oil and concrete, electric power and motor vehicles. Soviet military capacity was estimated in the present and projected into the future; the picture—of two hundred atomic bombs by 1954—was deeply disturbing.

The alert reader—the statistics, for all their purposefully shocking character, eventually glazed the eyes—caught on that there was a point to all this. After twenty thousand words and a couple of deliberately blind alleys—leading hypothetically to American surrender or an earth-shattering war—the paper laid out the only feasible course of action: a major program of American rearmament. No specific multiple of current spending was recommended, but in an emergency "an increase of several times present expenditures" wasn't out of the question. After all, during the recent world war the United States had devoted more than 50 percent of its gross national product to defense and related purposes. The current crisis was no less dangerous. "The cold war is in fact a real war in which the survival of the free world is at stake." Under the circumstances anything less than an all-out effort was irresponsible and dangerous.[7]

THE CAPITULATION OF THE CONSERVATIVES

Conservatives certainly would have objected to parts of NSC-68 had they been allowed to read it. But the report was immediately stamped "top secret" and withheld from public scrutiny — for nearly thirty years, as matters turned out. Naturally the gist of the paper surfaced soon enough — the exercise wasn't simply for the sake of the participants, who largely concurred with the conclusions even if some of them silently groaned at the apocalyptic language. The point of the exercise, as Dean Acheson later conceded, was "to so bludgeon the mass mind of 'top government' that not only could the President make a decision but that the decision could be carried out." The decision in question was to enlarge the military forces of the United States by two or three times; carrying the decision out required persuading Congress to front the money.[8]

Whether Acheson's bludgeon would have sufficed is an interesting historical question; in the event, the administration received additional timely assistance from the Communist camp. The NSC paper was hardly back from the printer when North Korean troops rolled across the Thirty-eighth Parallel and smashed the defenses of South Korea. In the context of the time it appeared patent that Kim Il Sung had the approval, if not the spur, of Moscow and Beijing; world communism was on the march just as NSC-68 had foretold. This new evidence of the danger confronting democracy flabbergasted even those who had been so breathless on paper just weeks before. The Truman administration, which earlier in the year had declared Korea beyond the pale of America's security perimeter, now felt compelled to throw American forces into the breach. With stunning suddenness Americans found their country at war once again.

But it wasn't a real war — at least not a congressionally declared war. And this, as much as anything else, was what bothered the conservatives. Truman was clever — and lucky. His luck followed from the historical peculiarity that Republican conservatives who roundly rejected American responsibility for the security of Europe often adopted a proprietary attitude toward Asia. This fact wasn't politically inexplicable: especially since the Communist victory in China just the previous autumn, the Democrats were much more vulnerable on Asian affairs than European. At the same time, it reflected certain personal circumstances — the upbringing in China of Republican magazine magnate Henry Luce, for instance. In any case Truman cannily recognized that those conservatives who might have faulted him for playing loose with the Constitution in conducting a war without congressional authorization would probably bite their tongues while he defended South Korea against Communist aggression. The president facilitated the tongue-biting by throwing an American cordon around Taiwan, where the poster boy of the Asia-firsters, Chiang Kai-shek, was making his last stand.

Between them, Kim Il Sung and Truman neatly cut the ground from beneath the feet of the conservatives. By acquiescing in Truman's decision to send U.S. forces into battle, the conservatives essentially surrendered their right to criticize the Cold War paradigm on philosophical grounds. To be sure, they would flail Truman on tactical issues, as Joseph McCarthy — hardly a true conservative but often mistaken for one — did in saying of the president that "the son-of-a-bitch must have been drunk on bourbon and benedictine" when he fired General MacArthur for insubordination in the conduct of the Korean war. But in embracing the defense of Korea, the conservatives bought into the Cold War.[9]

The terms of the conservative surrender became evident during the first winter of the war. After an initial period of alarm for Korea's sake — alarm amplified in the autumn of 1950, when China entered the war — the deepest concern of U.S. officials was that the Soviets would take advantage of America's entanglement in Asia to jump the West in Germany. It was this concern that led the Truman administration to propose sending a permanent garrison force of four U.S. divisions to Europe.

At the time of Senate debate on the North Atlantic treaty, the administration had countered conservative objections that it would lead to something like the present proposed troop deployment by disclaiming any such thoughts. Now that it was caught in its deception — or lack of foresight, to put an unwarrantedly charitable gloss on the matter — conservatives might have been expected to assail the White House as unmercifully as they were doing on several other fronts. But their attack was surprisingly subdued. To be sure, Robert Taft gave a long speech in the Senate casting doubt on the administration's prudence in seeking the deployment; he said the Soviets didn't want war, that the deployment would be a provocation and of course expensive to boot, that the Europeans ought to learn to defend themselves, and not least, that the president had no constitutional authority to send American troops overseas in peacetime. To a friend he reiterated his earlier warning about the inevitable connection between big government at home and big government overseas: "We seem to be stepping from the welfare state into the garrison state."[10]

But not even Taft could resist the consensus that had coalesced around the Cold War. When compromisers fashioned an amendment that would give the president his four divisions but require him to obtain congressional approval for further troops, Taft joined thirty-seven other Republicans in supporting the measure.

Whether or not the dispatch of the American divisions to Europe in 1951 was a provocation, as Taft warned, it certainly wasn't what conservatives and nearly everyone else in America had anticipated at the end of World War II. At that time the overwhelming expectation was that American troops would be coming home, not going back overseas. And in keeping with historical precedent, the swollen government of the wartime years would surely shrink back toward its peacetime norm. Briefly these expectations began to be realized.

But the onset of the Cold War halted the process, then reversed it. The United States prepared for war, first emotionally, then politically and militarily. It created a national-security bureaucracy that dwarfed anything Americans had tolerated before in peacetime, and it rebuilt the armed forces it had so recently hastened to dismantle. By the early 1950s it was fighting one war in Asia and girding for another in Europe. Under the circumstances, opponents of an active foreign policy had about as much credibility as opponents of World War II after Pearl Harbor; not surprisingly, they were almost as rare.

4 LIBERALS ALL!

The tide of postwar liberalism reached the flood stage during the 1960s, but the waves had been lapping higher for some time. As long as the Democrats controlled both the executive and legislative branches of government (which was to say from 1933 until 1947), the New Deal remained tenuous and provisional. Republicans routinely promised to repeal the Wagner Act, Social Security, and the various other manifestations of creeping statism. After seizing Congress following the 1946 elections, they did manage to weaken the Wagner law, and they fairly well strangled Truman's Fair Deal. But Truman's unexpectedly tenacious grip on the White House placed the counterrevolution on hold for another four years.

Oddly—or so it seemed to many at the time—the Republican conquest of the White House in the 1952 election led not to a rollback of the New Deal but to the New Deal's entrenchment. Dwight Eisenhower was a Cold War Republican, one of the first of the breed. By his own account—which of course may not have been the whole account—he entered the race in 1952 only because he feared that a Taft nomination and victory would lead to the undoing of NATO and a return to the isolationism of the interwar period.

Domestic affairs initially took second place in his thinking. Yet no president could ignore domestic issues, and once he defeated Taft — and then Adlai Stevenson — and cemented the American commitment to the Cold War, he inevitably turned to the home front. Eisenhower never became a New Dealer, but his understanding that the Cold War was a comprehensive threat to the American way of life inclined him toward a comprehensive response, one that went beyond traditional notions of defense to areas of national life previously considered simply domestic. Social Security fell easily into his compass of what a modern government ought to involve itself in; so, with greater or less difficulty, did an expanded federal role in transportation, education, and civil rights.

The liberalism of John Kennedy and Lyndon Johnson was more predictable, as, by their turn in office, was the appeal to the Cold War as justification for domestic reform. The early 1960s witnessed a proliferation of independence in the lately colonial regions of the world. As U.S. officials pondered how to win the respect and support of the predominantly poor and nonwhite people of Asia, Africa, and Latin America, they realized they would improve their chances by improving the prospects of poor and nonwhite people in the United States. The American creed had historically included equal rights and opportunities for all; during the 1960s Americans felt increasing pressure to redeem the promises of that creed.

By no stretch of the imagination was the Cold War the single, or even the primary, cause of the civil rights movement or the War on Poverty. Millions of Americans found racial and economic inequality sufficiently noxious that they needed no external inducement to attack it. But it wasn't an accident that the high tide of liberalism coincided with the high tide of America's participation in the Cold War. The Cold War caused Americans to look at their country through the eyes of others, and it raised the perceived costs to the nation as a whole of a continuation of an illiberal status quo. At the same time, the imperatives of the Cold War provided political cover for many who might otherwise have had difficulty supporting challenges to that status quo. Most fundamentally, by fostering reliance on the federal government in the area of national security, the Cold War encouraged a tendency to look to the federal government in other areas, and the confidence in government that the successful prosecution of the Cold War engendered spilled over into the domestic arena.

WE'RE NOT IN KANSAS ANY MORE, GENERAL

When Eisenhower gained the presidency in January 1953, the Cold War was entering a new phase. Both superpowers were on the verge of deploying thermonuclear weapons, which were to the bombs that devastated Hiroshima and Nagasaki what those bombs were to conventional weapons. Both sides were rapidly extending the range of their bomber fleets, which were designed to deliver these horrific weapons upon the industrial and population centers of the other. Both sides were developing long-range rockets, which would deliver the bombs even faster and would preclude any meaningful defense. When Eisenhower, as a boy in Kansas in the late 1890s, had begun to ponder a career at arms, the state of the military art—exemplified by the 1898 conflict with Spain—was in many respects much as it had been for centuries. Combatants still met each other directly and, for the most part, avoided inflicting casualties on noncombatants. Wars typically had distinct beginnings, marked by formal declarations of belligerence, and definite ends, treaties of peace. War was war, peace was peace, and if the twain met, they did so only briefly.

The Cold War could hardly have been more different. The United States was nominally at peace with the Soviet Union, but one wouldn't have known it from the hostility that infused U.S.-Soviet relations and from the war preparations each side was making. At the beginning of 1953 American forces were actively fighting North Korean and Chinese Communists; should this count as part of the struggle against the Soviet Union? Most Americans thought so. If a regular war did break out against Moscow, the traditional rules of warfare would almost certainly go by the boards at once. The monster new weapons would annihilate civilians by the millions; such vaporizing of cities was their only purpose. The soldiers — if that was the right word — who commanded the weapons would never see those they killed; they might never even see the battlefield — if *that* was the right word.

Eisenhower hadn't expected things to turn out this way when he left Abilene for West Point, and half a century later, having personally witnessed the destruction even conventional weapons could now wreak, he was appalled at what war had become. Yet he saw no way out of this technological cul-de-sac; and indeed his actions as president drove the nation farther down the nuclear dead end.

Shortly after taking office, Eisenhower directed his military planners to figure out how to maintain America's strategic superiority without bankrupting the country. Their solution, which he readily embraced, was the New Look, a defense posture that increased America's reliance on nuclear weapons while diminishing the role of conventional weapons. The great advantage of nuclear weapons was that they delivered "more bang for the buck," in the terminology of the time. The great disadvantage was that they tended to magnify small crises into large ones. Initially the president and his advisers sought to portray this tendency as an advantage. Secretary of State John Foster Dulles boasted of the "massive retaliatory power" of American nuclear weapons and explained that the president had made a "basic decision . . . to depend primarily upon a great capacity to retaliate, instantly, by means and at places of our choosing." No longer would the United States have to fight the Communists where the Communists wanted to fight; instead the nation could focus its attention on the center of the worldwide Communist conspiracy: Moscow.[1]

But many people weren't convinced. What the administration seemed to be saying was that any small provocation just about anywhere could be the trigger for a major nuclear war. Did Eisenhower really intend to risk Armageddon over some jungle brouhaha in some godforsaken Asian backwater? The administration's response was that the mere threat of American retaliation would compel the Kremlin to keep its agents in line. Maybe so — but what if some guerrilla leader somewhere didn't get the message?

Eisenhower had an answer to this question as well, although he didn't detail the answer in public. First among postwar presidents, Eisenhower authorized a regular campaign of covert warfare against foreign factions and governments deemed threatening to American interests but not so threatening as to warrant a formal American declaration of war. The covert operations ran the gamut from unacknowledged propaganda to secret warfare and assassination plots. Eisenhower wasn't particularly proud of this aspect of his administration's strategy in fighting the Cold War, but he judged that it came with the territory of battling communism. In 1954 he appointed General James Doolittle, the World War II flying hero, to assess America's covert capacities and performance; Doolittle summarized the rationale for the sub rosa operations: "If the United States is to survive, long-standing American concepts of 'fair play' must be reconsidered. We must develop effective espionage and counter-espionage services and must learn to subvert, sabotage and destroy our enemies by more clever, more sophisticated, and more effective methods than those used against us."[2]

Eisenhower agreed, and he quietly promoted covert operations as an essential aspect of American foreign policy. Under Eisenhower the Central Intelligence Agency helped topple Mohammed Mosadeq, the nationalist prime minister of Iran, in favor of the more reliably pro-American Shah; it assisted in the ouster of Jacobo Arbenz of Guatemala, another nationalist who threatened a pro-American status quo; and it engaged in a variety of less successful (from Washington's perspective) activities designed to destabilize enemies and succor friends. It also conducted garden-variety espionage—something the United States government, before 1945, had never done on a regular basis except in wartime.

Americans at large knew none of the specifics of the covert campaign. But through judicious leaks by CIA director Allen Dulles and others they gathered enough of the generalities to be able to conclude that their government was working busily behind the scenes to keep them secure. The formula was ideal for fostering faith in government. American officials said, in essence: Trust us. We'd tell you more, but we can't without weakening our defenses against those diabolical Communists.

Americans had little alternative to accepting this explanation—and little reason to question it. A person didn't have to be a raving McCarthyite to be concerned about Communist subversion. There really *were* Communist spies, at least according to the standards of

Anglo-American jurisprudence. And what Klaus Fuchs, Alger Hiss, and the Rosenbergs had given away wasn't sawdust. Moreover, as Jimmy Doolittle correctly noted, the Communists had no qualms about playing dirty; didn't democracy have the right to defend itself? Americans had trusted their government to defend democracy during World War II. They had refrained from prying too deeply into the details of military operations, and their trust had been rewarded with a brilliant success that had saved the world from fascism. The current struggle seemed an extension of that earlier one; it was democracy versus totalitarianism once again. National safety dictated continued reliance on those in charge.

Eisenhower's adoption of the New Look reinforced this reliance. With American security resting on a relatively small number of ultra-sophisticated weapons, the role of scientific expertise and top-secret intelligence assumed critical importance. What was the precise nature of the Soviet threat? How many bombers did the Russians have? How many rockets? What kinds of weapons did the United States require to defend itself? Laypersons could never hope to answer these questions by themselves, and even experts, unless they had access to government intelligence sources, were hardly better off. Government knew best — if only because no one else, compared to government, knew much of anything at all.

And the massive-retaliation policy of nuclear deterrence exaggerated the war mentality that had been part of the Cold War from the beginning. Even at the height of World War II, for those Americans not on the front lines the immediate physical danger from the enemy was essentially nonexistent. Now obliteration could come at any moment, literally as a bolt from the blue. Cultural critics then and later derided the Eisenhower era as a time of suffocating conformism, an extended season of the bland leading the bland. But that is exactly what one would expect of a people under threat of imminent destruction. In wartime, individualism is hardly a prized commodity. The collective welfare takes precedence.

WAGING PEACE

Eisenhower's liberalism was a response to just this sort of thinking. By instinct Eisenhower was a conservative; as president he constantly fretted that big government would disrupt the working of the American market economy, and he endlessly lectured his cabinet and anyone else who would listen on the need to balance the federal budget. At times even members of his own administration thought he was carrying his cost cutting to extremes. "If we ever go to the American people and tell them that we are putting a balanced budget ahead of national defense," warned Defense Secretary Charles Wilson at a moment when Eisenhower's New Look seemed to many to be doing just that, "it would be a terrible day."[3]

Nevertheless, Eisenhower, having spent almost his entire adult life working for the federal government, wasn't as completely convinced as some of his conservative friends that Washington would screw up anything it set its hand to. He was also realistic enough to recognize that once people had come to expect government to assume certain responsibilities, shedding those responsibilities would be painful—to the people themselves and to whatever party prompted the shedding. "Should any political party attempt to abolish social security and eliminate labor laws and farm programs, you would not hear of that party again in our political history," he wrote his brother Edgar. The president recognized that some Republicans — including Edgar — advocated just such abolition. But he didn't take them seriously. "Their number is negligible and they are stupid."[4]

Eisenhower had more respect for the captain-of-industry types with which he filled his cabinet. Yet these were no swashbuckling Harrimans and Carnegies and Rockefellers. Defense Secretary Wilson, formerly president of General Motors, best exemplified the new model of corporate executives who had made their peace with the welfare state and were making their profits with the Cold War — in some cases directly, in some cases from the overall prosperity the Cold War rearmament helped spur. (This prosperity came as no surprise to those who ordered the rearmament program. The authors of NSC-68 had predicted: "The economic effects of the program might be to increase the gross national product by more than the amount being absorbed for additional military and foreign assistance purposes. One of the most significant lessons of our World War II experience was that the American economy, when it operates at a level approaching full efficiency, can provide enormous resources for purposes other than civilian consumption while simultaneously providing a high standard of living.") As executives like Wilson recognized, Social Security, unemployment insurance, and other federal guarantees to workers helped stabilize the labor force and eased demands for programs that corporations might otherwise have had to pay for themselves. In any event, during a period of economic growth such costs as these programs created for businesses could be passed along to consumers.[5]

Eisenhower didn't disagree with the liberalism-as-social-stabilizer argument. Indeed, not content with defending Social Security against conservative attack, he insisted that the program be enlarged. At his prodding Congress raised benefits to recipients and extended coverage to some 10 million people previously excluded.

But Eisenhower was more persuaded by the liberalism-as-national-security argument — an argument that led him to support projects that wouldn't have passed his muster on their domestic merits alone. A modest example was the St. Lawrence seaway. Many Republicans — and more than a few Democrats — wondered why the president placed such priority on completing the series of locks and canals that would facilitate ship traffic between the Great Lakes and the Atlantic. Conservatives who still daydreamed of dynamiting dams of the Tennessee Valley Authority looked on the St. Lawrence project as another federal boondoggle. But Eisenhower closely heeded studies indicating that the mother lode of American iron ore, the Mesabi range of Minnesota, would fail before long, leaving the steelmakers of the Great Lakes — and the American arms makers who needed the steel to fabricate their weapons — dependent on ore from abroad. The St. Lawrence seaway would ensure that this ore found its way to the blast furnaces and rolling mills and thence to the ship hulls and artillery barrels. For Eisenhower the national-security argument provided just the hammer to beat down the budget hawks, and he pounded the appropriation through Congress.

Eisenhower's support of the interstate highway system revealed similar considerations. In the decade since Detroit had reconverted from tanks and planes to cars, Americans had taken to the highways with a vengeance — almost literally, in consequence of the inadequacy of roads that hadn't been updated since before the Great Depression and that now exacted an alarming toll of fatal mishaps. As a country boy, Eisenhower appreciated what good roads could mean to those who had to travel long distances to markets and towns. But as a Republican he appreciated how much the roads cost, and how roads and highways had been chiefly the responsibility of the states.

What tipped the balance for Eisenhower was the argument that good roads would enhance national defense. At a time when the threat of Soviet air attack was growing, and when anti-aircraft defenses were unreliable and anti-missile defenses nonexistent, the only hope of materially reducing civilian casualties in the event of general war was to evacuate targeted cities. The proposed new highways — four-lane, limited-access roads without stoplights or other obstructions — would move people out of cities many times faster than the current tangle of roads left over from the horse-and-buggy era. Moreover, the federal responsibility for this aspect of the program was irrefutable. Since the eighteenth century national defense had been a federal responsibility; it remained so — more than ever.

Was the Cold War therefore responsible for what turned out to be the largest public-works project in world history? Not by itself. Concrete makers, truckers, property owners along likely rights-of-way, congressmen from congested suburbs — these and dozens of other interest groups had their own reasons for supporting the interstate system, reasons that had nothing to do with the danger of Russian air raids. But major legislation always subsumes a congeries of motives — and almost always generates substantial opposition. In this case the defenders of the status quo, including not simply taxpayers' advocates and philosophical anti-federalists but also railroad executives and railroad unions and barge and pipeline owners and other groups that expected to be damaged by competition from the new highways, had been holding off the road gangs for years. The Cold War was the new element in the situation, and it provided just the additional argument needed to bulldoze the opposition and get the graders going.

The connection between the Cold War and another manifestation of Eisenhower-era liberalism was more straightforward. From the start of his administration the president had resisted conservative demands to cut federal aid to education. At one early cabinet meeting the secretary of Health, Education, and Welfare, Oveta Culp Hobby, unveiled plans to trim spending on schools. Eisenhower objected at once. "I am amazed at the thought of an education cut!" he told the assembled group. "This is the most important thing in our society." Looking straight at Hobby, he declared, "Every liberal — including me — will disapprove." Yet, liberal or not, Eisenhower at first wasn't prepared to *expand* federal aid to education, citing budgetary restrictions and the long-standing tradition of local and state responsibility for education.[6]

But early in his second term the Cold War erased his qualms — along with those of millions of other Americans. In October 1957 the Soviet Union launched the first successful artificial earth satellite. Sputnik amazed the world and stunned Americans, who until then had complacently assumed that their country enjoyed a secure scientific lead over the Communists. The implications of Sputnik were sobering: a political system that could launch a satellite clear around the earth could soon — if not already — launch a warhead halfway around the earth from Russia to the United States. Not only was American prestige on the line; so was American security.

Besides predictably sparking demands for increased spending on defense and space exploration, the Sputnik scare made liberals out of nearly everyone on the education issue. Congress immediately began searching for ways to produce scientists and engineers who would equal Russia's. Hearings hadn't even started before it became obvious that the legislature would order a major package of aid to scientific and technical education; the only question was the size and shape of the package. Eisenhower found himself in the congenial— for a Republican president—position of acting as a brake on the more liberal designs of Democrats on Capitol Hill. But when all the maneuvering and negotiating ended in August 1958, the National Defense Education Act authorized the spending of nearly $1 billion over four years—$1 billion that almost certainly would not have been spent absent the spur of the Cold War.

If Eisenhower had to be nudged into greater federal activism on education, he had to be dragged kicking and screaming into a larger role on race. His reluctance here may have reflected what he had learned in school of the history of his home state: how race had made "bleeding Kansas" the first battlefield of the Civil War. Perhaps the Kansas origins of the seminal 1954 Supreme Court case, *Brown v. Board of Education of Topeka,* somehow contributed to his determination to keep hands off. For whatever reasons, for three years after *Brown* he essentially left race matters alone.

But the cost of avoiding the issue increased with passing time. The 1955 Montgomery bus boycott brought Jim Crow—and Martin Luther King, Jr.—to national attention. More to the point for Eisenhower, it brought the American race problem to international attention. Foreign visitors had long remarked on the discrepancy between the rhetoric of American equality and the practice of American discrimination. But as the European colonial empires crumbled after 1945 and the new states of Asia and Africa gained independence and sent representatives to Washington and the United Nations in New York, America's racial situation grew more embarrassing than ever. It also grew potentially dangerous to American national interests. Lawyers for the Justice Department had made this argument in the Brown case. "The existence of discrimination against minority groups in the United States has an adverse effect upon our relations with other countries," asserted the department's amicus brief. "Racial discrimination furnishes grist for the Communist propaganda mills." Eisenhower's U.N. ambassador, Henry Cabot Lodge, stressed the point repeatedly in letters to the president. "At the United Nations General Assembly," Lodge declared, "you see the world as a place in which a large majority of the human race is non-white. The non-white majority is growing every year, as more African states gain their independence." Lodge asserted that the United States would have great difficulty winning the allegiance of the new nations unless it could demonstrate its bona fides on the issue of racial equality.[7]

The problem of world opinion grew critical during the autumn of 1957, when Governor Orval Faubus of Arkansas obstructed the implementation of federal integration orders at Little Rock's Central High School. Lodge was dismayed. "Here at the United Nations I can see clearly the harm that the riots in Little Rock are doing to our foreign relations," he wrote. Once again he urged the president to demonstrate the nation's commitment to racial equality.[8]

Eisenhower was as reluctant as before to involve the federal government in what he considered social engineering, but the Little Rock resistance left him no choice. How could the government of the United States lead the Free World if it couldn't enforce its authority within the United States? In announcing his decision to send federal troops to Little Rock, Eisenhower made plain that he personally didn't agree with court-ordered integration, yet he went on to say that "our personal opinions about the decision have no bearing on the matter of enforcement." The responsibility and authority of the Supreme Court to interpret the Constitution were "very clear," as was the duty of the executive branch to uphold the Court's ruling. The Little Rock matter had the most serious implications not only for public order in the United States but for the fate of freedom around the world.

> At a time when we face grave situations abroad because of the hatred that Communism bears toward a system of government based on human rights, it would be difficult to exaggerate the harm that is being done to the prestige and influence, and indeed to the safety, of our nation and the world.
>
> Our enemies are gloating over this incident and using it everywhere to misrepresent our whole nation. We are portrayed as a violator of those standards of conduct which the peoples of the world united to proclaim in the Charter of the United Nations. There they affirmed "faith in fundamental human rights" and "in the dignity and worth of the human person" and they did so "without distinction as to race, sex, language or religion."
>
> And so, with deep confidence, I call upon the citizens of the State of Arkansas to assist in bringing to an immediate end all interference with the law and its processes. If resistance to the Federal Court orders ceases at once, the further presence of Federal troops will be unnecessary and the City of Little Rock will return to its normal habits of peace and order and a blot upon the fair name and high honor of our nation in the world will be removed.[9]

Diehard segregationists scoffed at Eisenhower's appeal to patriotism and national security; some even turned the argument around, calling the president a Hitler and a Stalin for employing military force against American citizens. But for those many in the middle on the race question — those who would ultimately determine the outcome of the struggle against the segregationist system — the linking of civil rights to America's fortunes in the Cold War provided a powerful new argument for racial equality.

THE NEW FRONTIER THESIS

John Kennedy made the link between liberalism and the Cold War explicit from the beginning of his administration. "Let every nation know," he announced at his inauguration, "whether it wishes us well or ill, that we shall pay any price, bear any burden, meet any hardship, support any friend, oppose any foe to assure the survival and success of liberty." This was the Cold Warrior speaking, but the liberal quickly chimed in. "If a free society cannot help the many who are poor, it cannot save the few who are rich." Kennedy made a particular pledge to the nations of the Western Hemisphere, lately beguiled by the Castro revolution in Cuba; the United States would "assist free men and free governments in casting off the chains of poverty." To the world at large he extended a promise of cooperation in the "struggle against the common enemies of man: tyranny, poverty, disease and war."

Like Eisenhower — and every other Cold War president — Kennedy perceived an intimate connection between what Americans did abroad and what they did at home. On behalf of his "new generation of Americans" he asserted a national refusal "to witness or permit the slow undoing of those human rights to which this nation has always been committed, and to which we are committed today at home and around the world." The same spirit of endeavor that must motivate Americans domestically would energize the advocates of freedom overseas. "My fellow Americans: ask not what your country can do for you—ask what you can do for your country. My fellow citizens of the world: ask not what America will do for you, but what together we can do for the freedom of man."[10]

Kennedy marched boldly forward in both foreign and domestic affairs. In April 1961 he ordered the invasion of Cuba at the Bay of Pigs by a small contingent of CIA-trained and -supported anti-Castro exiles. The operation immediately exploded in his face, failing spectacularly and convincing him to be more circumspect in the future, although not necessarily more cautious. He set aside further invasion plans in favor of attempts to assassinate Castro.

The Bay of Pigs fiasco encouraged Nikita Khrushchev to try to slip some Soviet nuclear missiles into Cuba. When discovered by American spy satellites in the autumn of 1962, the Cuban missiles provoked the most terrifying hundred hours in the history of the Cold War. Americans clustered around their television sets—those who weren't digging bomb shelters in their backyards—to determine whether Kennedy's demand for the missiles' withdrawal and his imposition of an anti-Soviet blockade of Cuba would trigger the holocaust many had feared from the beginning of the Cold War. To the relief of the world, Khrushchev accepted Kennedy's public promise not to invade Cuba and his private pledge to withdraw U.S. missiles from Turkey, and pulled the Russian rockets out of Cuba.

Kennedy emerged from the crisis as the model Cold Warrior: the cool but implacable foe of communism. Although some Americans, and doubtless a larger percentage of foreigners, wondered whether it had been strictly necessary to push to the brink of nuclear war to restore the strategic status quo in the Caribbean, Kennedy's performance won him the plaudits of his compatriots. His approval rating jumped sharply: from 62 percent in the last Gallup poll before the crisis to 74 percent in the first one afterward. Americans were reminded, in terms that could scarcely have been more arresting, that the world was a dangerous place, and most were willing to accept that their safety required decisive action by their government.[11]

It was Kennedy's belief, and again one that most Americans seemed willing to accept, that similar decisiveness was required in domestic affairs. In April 1962 the United States Steel Corporation announced a price increase of 3.5 percent in its basic product line; within days the other major steel firms followed suit. Kennedy had spent the previous months jawboning steelworkers to keep their wage demands below the 3 percent guidelines established by his Council of Economic Advisers to restrain inflation; the steel unions, complaining that their members had already lost ground but unwilling to defy a popular Democratic president, grumblingly agreed. Kennedy hardly had time to savor his victory before the steel corporations unveiled their price hike, which implicitly made him seem a shill for U.S. Steel and its fellow oligopolists. Privately he muttered, "My father always told me that all businessmen were sons of bitches, but I never believed it till now." To the nation he decried the price hike as "a wholly unjustifiable and irresponsible defiance of the public interest."

In particular, the actions of the steel companies jeopardized American security. "In this serious hour in our nation's history," Kennedy declared, "when we are confronted with grave crises in Berlin and Southeast Asia . . . when we are asking reservists to leave their homes and families for months on end and servicemen to risk their lives — and four were killed in the last two days in Vietnam — . . . at a time when restraint and sacrifice are being asked of every citizen, the American people will find it hard, as I do, to accept a situation in which a tiny handful of steel executives whose pursuit of private power and profit exceeds their sense of public responsibility can show such utter contempt for the interests of 185 million Americans." Kennedy explained that the Defense Department had calculated what the steel hike would cost the country's military. "It would add, Secretary McNamara informed me this morning, an estimated $1 billion to the cost of our defenses, at a time when every dollar is needed for national security and other purposes." Besides the direct cost to weapons purchases, the hike would make it more difficult for the government to improve the American balance of trade and to stem the outflow of American gold. The gold drain was especially troublesome. "It is necessary to stem it for our national security, if we're going to pay for our security commitments abroad."[12]

With the nation's security at risk, the president felt justified in bringing the full weight of the federal government to bear to force a repeal. He announced investigations by the Justice Department and the Federal Trade Commission into potentially criminal price-fixing in the steel industry. He ordered the Pentagon to review its procurement practices; the public's business would be steered away from the offending firms. Administration allies in Congress launched their own probes; special legislation, which would certainly not favor the big steel companies, was a strong possibility.

The steel executives, unaccustomed to public pillory for lack of patriotism and reckless disregard of national security, folded in the face of Kennedy's counterattack. Within days they capitulated and rescinded their price hike.

It had been an formidable display of executive power. The price controls of the world wars had lapsed long before, but Kennedy insisted on reimposing them, in effect, against one of the most powerful industries in the country. Needless to say, conservatives wailed. The *Wall Street Journal* blistered the president's cavalier use of "naked power"; the Republican congressional leadership warned darkly of "police state methods." The president of the American Chamber of Commerce declared, "We should remember that dictators in other lands usually come to power under accepted constitutional procedures."[13]

Kennedy shrugged off the criticism, expecting no better from those S.O.B.'s of the boardrooms. He had a harder time ignoring another response from Wall Street: the collapse of the stock market a month later. Not since 1929 had stocks tumbled so alarmingly. Naturally conservatives and other Kennedy critics laid the swoon on the doorstep of the White House.

Kennedy wasn't willing to accept the blame, but neither could he ignore the ominous portents of the stock dive for the economy. In 1962 the country wasn't so far from the Great Depression that Americans couldn't recall how the last such stock plunge had ushered in a decade of economic and social distress and contributed to World War II. Kennedy's economic advisers, led by Walter Heller, had been urging him to employ the tools of Keynesian theory to stimulate the economy; while the president sympathized, until now he judged that the political costs of a stimulus package of budget deficits outweighed the economic benefits. But the stock crash demonstrated the downside of doing nothing, and he threw his support to the deficit squad.

Not completely: where Heller and the others advocated unbalancing the budget by raising spending, Kennedy chose to cut taxes. By itself the tax cut might have been taken as indicating a conservative shift — a curtailment of government activity. And, indeed, Kennedy soothed the jitters of the financial classes by presenting it in just such terms. In a speech to the Economic Club of New York he asserted, "The best means of strengthening demand among consumers and business is to reduce the burden on private income and the deterrents to private initiative which are imposed by our present tax system."[14]

But the proposed tax cut, far from signifying a retreat from government activism, really represented a signal advance. By embracing Keynesianism, Kennedy assumed on behalf of the federal government the responsibility for managing the national economy. For decades the connection between federal fiscal policy and the condition of the economy had been recognized, if not entirely agreed upon, but not until now had any administration openly claimed a mandate for manipulating tax and spending policies to spur the economy to faster growth. As before, Kennedy downplayed the liberal implications of his decision; he portrayed it as an essentially technical matter. "What is at stake in our economic decisions today," he told a commencement crowd at Yale University in June 1962, "is not some grand warfare of rival ideologies which will sweep the country with passion but the practical management of a modern economy. What we need is not labels and cliches but more basic discussion of the sophisticated and technical questions involved in keeping a great economic machinery moving ahead."[15]

Significantly, Kennedy justified both his proposed tax cut and what he saw as the overall federal responsibility for economic management in terms of national security. In his address to the New York Economic Club—delivered while the world was still getting over its nervousness from the Cuban missile crisis—he declared:

Less than a month ago this nation reminded the world that it possessed both the will and the weapons to meet any threat to the security of free men. The gains we have made will not be given up, and the course that we have pursued will not be abandoned. But in the long run, that security will not be determined by military or diplomatic moves alone. It will be affected by the decisions of finance ministers as well as by the decisions of Secretaries of State and Secretaries of Defense; by the deployment of fiscal and monetary weapons as well as by military weapons; and above all by the strength of this nation's economy as well as by the strength of our defenses.

Kennedy reminded the assembled bankers, brokers, and manufacturers that Khrushchev had predicted that history would turn decisively in socialism's direction when the Soviet economy outproduced the American. The world was watching to see if Khrushchev was right. For this reason, Kennedy explained, the health of the American economy involved "not merely our own well-being, but also very vitally the defense of the free world." Under such circumstances the federal government could not shirk responsibility for managing the economy.[16]

Kennedy's deliberate deficit had the anticipated effect of stimulating the economy, although he didn't live to see this vindication of the Keynesian gospel. Nor did he live to see the attainment of the most ambitious pledge of his administration, one that, perhaps better than any other, summarized both the intimate connection between foreign and domestic policy during the Cold War and the can-do spirit of 1960s liberalism. In May 1961 the president declared, "I believe that this nation should commit itself to achieving the goal, before this decade is out, of landing a man on the moon and returning him safely to earth." The context of Kennedy's challenge made plain that this was no disinterested call for expanding human knowledge of the cosmos. The space pledge was part of a special supplementary state-of-the-union message; the president acknowledged that state-of-the-union messages were traditionally annual affairs but added that the tradition had been broken in extraordinary times. He went on, "These are extraordinary times. And we face an extraordinary challenge. Our strength as well as our convictions have imposed upon this nation the role of leader in freedom's cause."

Most of Kennedy's address dealt with the nuts and bolts — literally, in the case of the new weaponry he requested — of national defense. Beyond the new helicopters, armored personnel carriers, and howitzers, he asked for increased funding for American "special forces" (notably the Green Berets), for American economic and military aid to friends and allies abroad, for counter-Communist informational activities, for civil defense (fallout shelters and the like), and for other activities traditionally within the realm of national defense. He also emphasized his theme of the centrality of a healthy economy to national defense; in this vein he proposed a manpower development and training program.

But as important as anything material was what America could do to win the moral support of those peoples beyond the superpower alliance systems. "The great battleground for the defense and expansion of freedom today is the whole southern half of the globe — Asia, Latin America, Africa and the Middle East — the lands of the rising peoples. Their revolution is the greatest in human history." American arms and American money could help these peoples defend themselves, but arms and money would not suffice. What was required additionally was a demonstration of the dynamism of the Free World. Unfortunately, recent events — especially the successful orbiting of the earth by Soviet cosmonaut Yuri Gagarin — suggested that the Soviet system was the one destined to dominate the future. "If we are to win the battle that is now going on around the world between freedom and tyranny, the dramatic achievements in space which occurred in recent weeks should have made clear to us all, as did the Sputnik in 1957, the impact of this adventure on the minds of men everywhere, who are attempting to make a determination of which road they should take." Kennedy didn't deny that the Russians currently had a lead in space technology, but he refused to surrender the heavens to the reds. "While we cannot guarantee that we shall one day be first, we can guarantee that any failure to make this effort will make us last. . . . We go into space because whatever mankind must undertake, free men must fully share."

Kennedy acknowledged the huge costs of the adventure he was proposing: up to $10 billion during the next six years alone. The effort would mirror, in many ways, the mobilization of wartime. "This decision demands a major national commitment of scientific and technical manpower, materiel and facilities, and the possibility of their diversion from other important activities where they are already thinly spread. It means a degree of dedication, organization and discipline which have not always characterized our research and development efforts." Neither scientists alone nor the government would be the ones putting that first American on the moon. "It will be an entire nation. For all of us must work to put him there." Only a united, national effort would enable the country to "move forward, with the full speed of freedom, in the exciting adventure of space."[17]

ALL THE WAY WITH LBJ

Along with much other unfinished business, Kennedy bequeathed the moon to Lyndon Johnson. The thirty-sixth president was as much a Cold War liberal as the thirty-fifth, but where Kennedy came to Cold War liberalism from the Cold War side, Johnson arrived from the liberal side. Kennedy reveled in the grand politics of war and peace and merely tolerated the pedestrian politics of bill-drafting and vote-counting; Johnson was just the opposite. Johnson's first love was legislating, his passion the flesh-and-blood business of cloakroom cajoling, the imploring, intimidating, berating, promising process of improving the lives of ordinary Americans by building a new school here, underwriting job training there, subsidizing rent across the street, paying for medical care around the corner. Johnson accepted the Cold War the way many people accept the religion of their parents: it explained prominent features of the world he inhabited, most of the people he knew believed in it, and he saw no reason to question it. But his foreign-affairs theology was strictly high church, whereas his domestic faith was tent-meeting revivalist. Brother Lyndon was born again in the gospel of government activism, and he devoted his career to spreading the good news.

The Great Society marked the apogee of American liberalism. The Civil Rights Act of 1964 and the Voting Rights Act of 1965 greatly expanded the federal reach on race. The Elementary and Secondary Education Act and the Higher Education Act put Washington in America's classrooms and on America's campuses as never before. The National Endowment for the Arts and the National Endowment for the Humanities appointed the federal government the sponsor of American arts and letters. Model Cities made the feds the architects and redevelopers of the nation's urban core. Medicare and Medicaid put the government in the health-care business. Head Start had it teaching toddlers. The War on Poverty aimed to redistribute some of the nation's wealth to the nation's neediest.

Certain of these measures were purely domestic, having nothing to do with foreign affairs or national defense. Not even the most ingenious Cold Warriors could figure out what the new national recreation areas had to do with American security, except perhaps to provide places for city-dwellers to flee to in the event of nuclear attack.

Yet many of the liberal programs *were* drawn into the Cold War nexus. Federal aid to elementary and secondary education had, among other purposes, a goal similar to that of the National Defense Education Act of the Eisenhower administration: to fashion the informed intelligences that would guarantee America's scientific and technological edge over the Communists. Johnson, in pushing for his educational bill, asserted that federal aid would enhance America's military strength. "Nothing matters more to the future of our country," he declared. Other programs would bolster the country analogously. The War on Poverty, for instance, would strengthen the economy, and hence the nation, by bringing the poor into the mainstream of economic life.[18]

Beyond this, the success of the Great Society would reinforce American security by demonstrating to the world that the American way of life was the one worth emulating. More than ever after the Cuban missile crisis, Americans understood that the struggle between ideological systems must not be by military means; rather it must be a contest to determine which system delivered the better life to its people. American prosperity had long been unchallenged, but until now America's commitment to equality was questionable. The Great Society would erase such questions, and in the process win the hearts and minds of those billions abroad who would ultimately render the verdict between democracy and communism.

In his state of the union address of January 1965, Johnson described the intimate link between liberalism at home and American security abroad. The United States, he declared, was "at the beginning of the road to the Great Society." The road was long; hence the nation needed to get started at once. "I propose that we begin a program in education to ensure every American child the fullest development of his mind and skills. I propose that we begin a massive attack on crippling and killing diseases. I propose that we launch a national effort to make the American city a better and a more stimulating place to live. I propose that we increase the beauty of America and end the poisoning of our rivers and the air that we breathe. I propose that we carry out a new program to develop regions of our country that are now suffering from distress and depression." And so on, through guaranteeing the right to vote, honoring and funding the arts, and eliminating the causes of crime and juvenile delinquency.

Why must the nation tackle this ambitious agenda? Partly for the good of Americans, to be sure. But also because the quality of life in America was indissolubly linked to the quality of life in the world, and the quality of life in the world had a direct bearing on American security. "Our concern and interest, compassion and vigilance, extend to every corner of a dwindling planet. . . . We were never meant to be an oasis of liberty and abundance in a worldwide desert of disappointed dreams. Our Nation was created to help strike away the chains of ignorance and misery and tyranny wherever they keep man less than God means him to be." At one time Americans had believed they could seek their salvation apart from the world, but no longer. Speaking a hundred years after the end of the war to save the Union, Johnson proclaimed that the United States must strive for a new, more perfect form of national unity, and he asserted, "The unity we seek cannot realize its full promise in isolation. For today the state of the Union depends, in large measure, upon the state of the world."[19]

Left to his own devices, Johnson might have desired that things were otherwise — that the state of the American union did *not* depend on the state of the world. Where Eisenhower had wished domestic problems like race would go away so he could concentrate on the Cold War, Johnson often wished the Cold War would go away so he could concentrate on domestic problems like race. But neither president got his wish, and both found the two sets of issues — the foreign and the domestic — irretrievably intertwined.

For Johnson the explicit connection was delayed; meanwhile he exploited the implicit connection. Nearly twenty years of Cold War had conditioned Americans to rely on the central government to solve their most serious problems, and nearly twenty years of comparatively consistent success in the Cold War had disposed Americans to trust that their government could accomplish what it set out to do. By the time Johnson entered office, a large reservoir of public confidence in government existed. Much of this confidence seemed, from outward appearances and on a day-to-day basis, to be independent of the Cold War and national security. Johnson, for one, cited national security as a justification for domestic liberalism far less often or explicitly than Eisenhower or Kennedy. In part this reflected the fact that, as a gut-level liberal himself, Johnson didn't need to be convinced that government activism was a good idea. No one who heard him respond to the violence against civil rights marchers at Selma, Alabama, by vowing before a joint session of Congress, "We *shall* overcome," could have had any doubt that Johnson's liberalism was a matter of the deepest personal conviction.

It was this deep personal conviction that led him to construe his responsibilities — and those of the federal government — so sweepingly. "I want to be the president who educated young children to the wonders of their world," Johnson told that same session of Congress.

> I want to be the President who helped to feed the hungry and to prepare them to be taxpayers instead of tax eaters. I want to be the President who helped the poor to find their own way and who protected the right of every citizen to vote in every election. I want to be the President who helped to end hatred among his fellow men and who promoted love among the people of all races, all regions and all parties. I want to be the President who helped to end war among the brothers of this earth.[20]

It was an astonishing agenda. That Johnson could confide it to Congress and the American people, and that Congress and the people could respond by giving him nearly everything he asked in the way of expanded federal power, demonstrated the degree to which government had come to be seen as the agent of first (or at least early) resort in solving social problems. Anomalous in the long scheme of their history, Americans' Cold War-inspired trust in government was what allowed Johnson's Great Society to take root.

Yet though he didn't often refer explicitly to the Cold War in promoting his programs, Johnson never forgot the linkage between foreign and domestic affairs. He fully understood that tending to the Cold War, in particular its current incarnation in Vietnam, was the cost of maintaining his ability to accomplish domestic reform. "I knew that if we let Communist aggression succeed in taking over South Vietnam," he later explained, "there would follow in this country an endless national debate — a mean and destructive debate — that would shatter my Presidency, kill my administration, and damage our democracy. I knew that Harry Truman and Dean

Acheson had lost their effectiveness from the day the Communists took over in China. I believed that the loss of China had played a large role in the rise of Joe McCarthy. And I knew that all these problems, taken together, were chickenshit compared with what might happen if we lost Vietnam."[21]

Of course Vietnam wouldn't have been Johnson's to lose if his Cold War predecessors hadn't staked American credibility on the survival of a non-Communist regime in Saigon. First Truman, then Eisenhower, then Kennedy had made Vietnam an American project; aid to France had transmuted into money and arms for Ngo Dinh Diem; American advisers had followed American arms; the advisers were followed in turn by American combat troops. Nothing worked for long, and Johnson found himself facing a choice between escalating the American commitment further and watching a decade-and-a-half of American effort, along with the attached prestige, collapse in ignominy. Johnson's orthodox view of the world included the anti-appeasement belief that aggression had to be halted at the outset wherever it occurred. Yet even if he hadn't bought into the philosophy of global containment, the commitment he inherited from Kennedy would have bound him politically, and he could hardly have done other than he did.

As it was, he sought desperately to keep Vietnam from derailing the Great Society. Despite growing chaos in Saigon after the overthrow and assassination of Diem (an ouster in which the frustrated Kennedy administration was deeply complicit), Johnson refused for more than a year to take strong action in Vietnam. He cast himself as the peace candidate, against the frightening — to judge by voters' response — Barry Goldwater, and he carefully cultivated congressional support for escalation, most notably via the Gulf of Tonkin resolution. Even after safely winning election in his own right, and after deciding escalation was unavoidable, he revealed his decision in careful (to the point of misleading) installments. He delayed large-scale bombing of North Vietnam until after he unveiled the four-score anti-poverty programs that would form the heart of the Great Society, and after he announced his intention to seek what became the Voting Rights Act. He procrastinated on major increases in ground troops until after winning approval of the voting act, Medicare, and the Elementary and Secondary Education Act. Throughout his presidency he refused to declare a national emergency, to call up the reserves, or to take any action, not absolutely necessary, that might jeopardize his domestic reforms.

Johnson appreciated the difficulty of his task. "If I left the woman I really loved — the Great Society — in order to get involved with that bitch of a war on the other side of the world," he reflected afterward, "then I would lose everything at home. All my programs. All my hopes to feed the hungry and shelter the homeless. All my dreams to provide education and medical care to the browns and the blacks and the lame and the poor. But if I left that war and let the Communists take over South Vietnam, then I would be seen as a coward and my nation would be seen as an appeaser and we would both find it impossible to accomplish anything for anybody anywhere on the entire globe."[22]

5

FROM HUBRIS TO SUTTEE

Johnson maintained his balancing act for four years. The Great Society was a brilliant legislative success, and in expanding the scope of government beyond anything most Americans had even conceived of ten years earlier, it set historic standards for liberalism. Whether it would be a social success — whether it would fulfill the promises Johnson and other liberals made on its behalf — would require years to determine, but if high hopes counted for anything, it was off to a rousing start.

Meanwhile the war in Vietnam proceeded more or less according to plan. Johnson had never expected a quick victory; indeed the essence of his strategy was not to vanquish the Communists but to outlast them, to demonstrate that each time Ho Chi Minh pushed more chips into the pot Lyndon Johnson would match him. This strategy had always been a gamble: Johnson was betting that the determination of Americans at least equaled that of the Vietnamese Communists. The bet — discounted on the American side for the much greater military power at America's disposal — had seemed a good one in 1964, and although the odds might have lengthened somewhat since then, the smart money was still on Washington.

"The war is going in our favor," CIA director Richard Helms told Johnson in November 1967.[1]

But the smarter money was on Hanoi. The Tet offensive of early 1968 revealed that the Communists had a great deal more fight left in them than most Americans had imagined, and even as American soldiers beat back the Communist advance, American morale at home suffered serious damage.

Just *how* serious wasn't immediately obvious. Although the Tet offensive blasted Johnson's hopes for another term in office, it allowed the election of Richard Nixon on a platform that, while deliberately vague, didn't encompass an abrupt end to the war. And it permitted Nixon to sustain the war effort through another four years and another twenty-five thousand American deaths.

Yet the damage proved to be insidious and pervasive. It drove Nixon to extraordinary measures of deception to keep the war going, and when the reality behind the deception became apparent, what was left of the Cold War consensus collapsed. Nixon had seen the end coming; his diplomacy of detente was a response to his recognition that the Cold War was no longer sustainable on its original terms. Yet for all his diplomatic deftness, his feet got tangled in the coils of his deception, and his administration came crashing down along with the Cold War consensus.

Liberals had never liked Nixon, even though from an operational standpoint he was one of them, and when his hubris brought him low, they piled on with glee. This may have been emotionally satisfying, but it was politically myopic. Liberals were slow to recognize that the demise of Cold War thinking in America vitiated what had consistently been one of their strongest arguments for reform, and they were largely blind to the fact that by helping destroy Nixon and discredit the institutions that allowed him to do what he did, they were driving a stake through the heart of the popular confidence in government on which Cold War liberalism had always rested.

BODY COUNTS, VOTE COUNTS

Opposition to the war after the Tet offensive hardly emerged out of thin air. Since the 1950s, critics of American policy in Indochina had been complaining that Washington was stretching the Munich analogy to the tearing point in trying to make it reach Southeast Asia. Because of the Republican party's historical weakness for Asian anti-Communists, most of the early critics were Democrats, and the arrival of Kennedy in the White House briefly quieted a large portion of the dissent. But few of the Kennedy partisans had much use for Johnson, who in turn harbored grave doubts about the "Harvards" and other East Coast intellectuals who crowded the court of Camelot, and as American operations in Vietnam escalated, so did the level of domestic opposition.

Yet the critics of the war were a motley crew. At the hard core of dissent were radicals of the New Left who rejected the Cold War as a manifestation of American militarism, and the war in Vietnam as an expression of that pernicious subgenre of American maleficence, imperialism. Mainstream critics of the war were far fewer at first, numbering in Congress—which by definition has always marked the mainstream of American politics—precisely two at the time of the 1964 Gulf of Tonkin resolution.

The bombing campaign of 1965 and the initiation of major American ground operations pushed more people into opposition.

Radicals still shouted the loudest, especially on campuses across the country, where opposition to the war was becoming intellectually and politically de rigueur. At the other end of the spectrum, conservatives of the Douglas MacArthur, no-substitute-for-victory school (which currently included as star scholar Air Force chief of staff Curtis LeMay, who complained that the peaceful outcome of the Cuban missile crisis represented a missed opportunity for American arms, and who advocated bombing North Vietnam "back to the Stone Age") lambasted the Johnson administration for forcing American soldiers to fight one-handed.[2]

As the toll in American lives mounted and victory kept being postponed, a few stalwarts of liberalism joined the opposition. Senators George McGovern and Eugene McCarthy criticized the bombing campaign, with McGovern's criticism carrying special weight as coming from a World War II bomber pilot. J. William Fulbright's Senate Foreign Relations Committee held televised hearings on the war in February 1966; these gave a forum and legitimacy to the dissenters. Even so, while public support for the war clearly wasn't what it had been, conventional wisdom at the end of 1967 held that a direct challenge to the president from within the Democratic party almost certainly meant political suicide for the challenger. Republicans, of course, were expected to challenge Johnson, but GOP front-runner Nixon, a red-baiter from the prehistory of the Cold War, hardly appeared the type to call off any anti-Communist action.

The Tet offensive changed everything. Coming after an autumn of optimism on the part of the administration, the Communist assault shook public confidence in American policy. The president's approval rating with respect to the war plummeted by a third, to a dismal 26 percent. What had seemed a quixotic quest by Eugene McCarthy to unseat the president suddenly assumed substance when New Hampshire Democrats gave him 42 percent of their votes — against 49 percent for Johnson — in that state's bellwether primary. McCarthy's moral victory enticed Robert Kennedy, a far more credible candidate, into the campaign. And then, to the shock of all but his closest confidants, Johnson threw the campaign wide open by canceling his own candidacy. At the same time the president signaled a fundamental change of course in Vietnam by suspending most of the bombing and declaring his intention to seek peace through negotiations.

DICK NIXON, FOR YOUR SINS

Richard Nixon read the opposition to the war perfectly. He understood that while Americans were weary of the war, as a group they weren't ready to walk away from fifteen years of struggle, twenty-five thousand lives lost, and tens of billions of dollars expended. They still wanted to win; they were simply questioning the cost of victory. And so, with either admirable optimism (according to his supporters) or supreme cynicism (in the judgment of his critics), Nixon promised a war-exit strategy that would square the cost-benefit circle that had defied all the rectifying energies of Johnson.

Considerations of patriotism (according to his supporters) or self-interest (his critics) prevented Nixon from sharing the details of his plan with voters before the election of 1968, but once Hubert Humphrey was safely defeated, he let the rest of the country in on "Vietnamization." The concept was simplicity itself: substitute South Vietnamese soldiers for Americans on the jungle patrols that were claiming so many lives. South Vietnam would do the heavy dying while the United States would provide air cover, logistical support, and all the weapons Saigon needed to defend itself.

The solution wasn't perfect. American taxpayers still had to pony up large sums of money; American pilots remained at risk of increasingly accurate North Vietnamese anti-aircraft crews; the capacity and morale of the South Vietnamese army had atrophied during years of dependence on the United States. Worst of all, there was absolutely no guarantee Vietnamization would work on the ground. If half a million U.S. troops hadn't been able to stabilize the situation in South Vietnam, how would Saigon's prospects improve when those soldiers were gone?

The answer, Nixon contended, lay in demonstrating American resolve. In this respect his strategy differed not in the slightest from Kennedy's or Johnson's: the Communists would lose heart when they discovered that they simply could not win. In Nixon's case this meant that Washington would supply whatever assistance — except U.S. foot soldiers — South Vietnam needed to keep fighting.

For Nixon to promise ceaseless support to Saigon was one thing; for Hanoi to *believe* his promises was something else. Besides being ruthlessly committed to the inevitability of the triumph of Marxism-Leninism, North Vietnamese leaders were skeptical that America would follow through on Nixon's commitment to Saigon. In light of the continuing domestic protests against the war, the Communists' skepticism was hardly unreasonable. Nixon understood this, and likewise understood the need to spike Hanoi's doubts.

It was to convince the Communists of American determination, as much as to gain some definite tactical benefits, that Nixon ordered the widening of the war into Cambodia and Laos. This American president, he signaled, would not let the formalities of national sovereignty shelter the enemies of freedom; those who took up arms against their neighbors would be hunted down wherever they hid.

The invasion of Cambodia in the spring of 1970 touched off the most widespread and violent domestic protests of the entire war. Nixon wasn't surprised. "I never had any illusions about the shattering effect a decision to go into Cambodia would have on public opinion at home," he remarked afterward — a statement whose veracity not even his critics questioned. But to Nixon's way of thinking, the public opposition was all the more reason for going ahead, for it would demonstrate even better America's determination, as he put it, "to protect ourselves and our allies."[3]

Nixon's shrewd estimate that the storm on the campuses would subside once classes let out for the summer proved accurate — in fact, the very intensity of the storm caused it to spend its force prematurely, as the protests closed many campuses ahead of schedule.

Yet Congress, unlike the colleges, didn't take a long summer break, and even though Nixon cast certain of his critics on Capitol Hill into the same "bum" category as the student protesters, they weren't as easy to ignore. The Senate repealed the Gulf of Tonkin resolution and approved a measure to cut off funds for the Cambodian operation. Even stronger measures — to force an American pullout from Southeast Asia entirely — were bruited. Nixon calculated that the House would stand up to this outbreak of dovishness: that the larger body, being accountable to voters every two years, would listen more carefully to the "silent majority" the president was counting on for continuing support.

Nixon reckoned accurately; the House did indeed rebuff the Senate's efforts to de-fund the war. Yet though he still had the votes in Congress, the president could see that they wouldn't be there forever. If he expected to succeed with his Vietnam policy, he needed help.

DETENTE AND ENJOY IT

Nixon looked for help in a place that flabbergasted both his friends and his foes. As it happened, the secret of the 1968 campaign was premised on an even deeper secret: that Nixon was counting on the Chinese and Soviets to make Vietnamization work. More than a decade before Ronald Reagan injected "supply side" into the lexicon of American politics, Nixon was a strategic supply-sider. He recognized that all the aid the United States might send to South Vietnam would be wasted if North Vietnam received offsetting aid from China and the Soviet Union; consequently, while filling to bursting the aid pipeline from Washington to Saigon, he sought to sever the lines from Beijing and Moscow to Hanoi.

Nixon's supply-side diplomacy was closely related to the basic insight of his presidency: that the Cold War had lost its metaphorical value. The Cold War had always been chiefly a figure of speech, of course; it wasn't really a war, cold or otherwise. In the late 1940s the concept had served the purpose of mobilizing the American people against the Soviet Union, and for the next twenty years it continued to serve that purpose. But the imagery of war had always been misleading, in that it implied that there would be a winner and a loser, and that — this being an ideological, and therefore moral, conflict as well as a geopolitical struggle — third parties ought to be required to choose sides. To be sure, American leaders often saw beyond the Cold War trope: as early as the Eisenhower administration, top officials in Washington made their private peace with the concept of Third World neutralism. But their public rhetoric, intended for America's Congress rather than India's Congress party, and for Cairo, Illinois, rather than Cairo, Egypt, limited their freedom of action and contributed to such paradoxical spectacles as John Foster

Dulles denouncing neutralism as "immoral" not long after chumming around the Adriatic with Yugoslavia's Tito, one of the founders of the nonaligned movement.[4]

Even more did the military metaphor of the Cold War limit American leaders in dealing with the fundamental fact of great-power relations during the 1960s: the falling-out—to the point of armed clashes—between China and the Soviet Union. The schism between the Communist giants afforded a fundamental opportunity for creative American diplomacy—but only if Americans could get past the bipolar thinking of the Cold War. Switching sides in a war has commonly been considered bad form: treacherous in the switcher and often at least embarrassing for the switchee. But side-switching is a standard feature of diplomacy, and rather than evoke condemnation or embarrassment, it usually elicits applause for the cleverness of the diplomats responsible.

Nixon was prepared to abandon the Cold War as an operative concept. Tension still existed between the United States and the Soviet Union, certainly, and would continue to exist. But tension was an inescapable part of intercourse among great powers. The central point was that, whatever its initial utility, the military mind-set that underpinned the Cold War had become counterproductive. The era of the Cold War had ended; the era of normalization must begin.

To be sure, no American politician who harbored any hopes of career advancement was about to declare the Cold War over at a time when victory couldn't credibly be claimed. What was required was a subtle reformulation, one that preserved some of the language of the Cold War yet made clear that the struggle for freedom had entered a new phase. The diplomatic term "detente" had been applied to postwar superpower relations intermittently during the

1950s, when it described the sporadic thawing between Moscow and Washington that followed the death of Stalin. The term went underground during the first couple of Kennedy years but resurfaced after the construction of the Berlin Wall solved the superpowers' central German problem, and after the Cuban missile crisis scared the daylights out of nearly everyone except Curtis LeMay. At first the West Europeans — particularly Charles de Gaulle of France and Willy Brandt of West Germany — led the detente forces on the NATO side, but by the last year of his presidency Lyndon Johnson had become a convert.

This meant, naturally, that Nixon had to keep his distance from the concept for a decent interval after the 1968 election. But in July 1971, Henry Kissinger, thought to be recuperating in Islamabad from a dinner his innards couldn't handle, turned up in Beijing. Kissinger's mere presence in the Chinese capital was astonishing enough; the national security adviser added to the shock value by announcing that his boss, the president, would be making the trip to the Forbidden City the following winter.

In earlier days, Nixon had often suggested it would be a cold day in hell before he paid Communist China the compliment of a visit. And on many occasions he had likened Red China to hell. So perhaps the cold weather was fitting when he arrived in Beijing in February 1971. But all was warmth and good cheer in the toasts and communiqués he exchanged with Mao Zedong — exchanges that marked an epoch in the affairs of the Pacific half of the planet.

Something decidedly different from good cheer was felt in Moscow at the sight of Nixon cavorting atop the Great Wall and pressing the flesh in Tiananmen Square. Naturally, this was the point of the cavorting and flesh-pressing. Nixon's China policy was part of his broader strategy of detente — part of his effort to create the structure of peace that would follow the Cold War. The international order of the Cold War had rested on two pillars: the United States and the Soviet Union. Nixon understood that the international order that followed the Cold War would rest on three pillars: the United States, the Soviet Union, and China.

The geometry of Nixon's post-Cold War order was impeccable: three-legged stools are inherently more stable than two-legged models. As it translated into foreign policy, the triangular structure of detente allowed Americans to participate in the kind of balance-of-power diplomacy that had characterized great-power relations for centuries.

The psychology of detente was trickier. Americans had never much cottoned to the idea of the balance of power, treating it as the kind of amoral manipulation that might suit Europe but not the exceptional republic on the Atlantic's western shore. Until the twentieth century America's standoffishness didn't much matter: the oceans remained nearly as wide as ever. World War I forced Americans to enter the game of nations, but that conflict — in particular, the outcome of that conflict — left a bad taste in American mouths that persisted until Pearl Harbor. World War II and the Cold War reinforced America's moralistic bent and seemed additionally to discredit the balance of power. Balancing power requires making compromises, acknowledging that one's adversaries today might be one's allies tomorrow.

This acknowledgment was precisely what Nixon was up to in China, and it was why he had gone to such lengths to shroud his China policy in secrecy. But after five years of heavy fighting in Vietnam, American moralism was momentarily exhausted; Nixon aimed to take advantage of this exhaustion to spring his China spectacular, which would dazzle the moralists long enough for the common sense of the new arrangement to sink in. Yet if word leaked out in advance, the moralists would rally once more against any accommodation of Red China, and would probably prevent it.

In 1947 the Truman doctrine had represented an effort to establish anti-Communist ideology as the basis of American foreign policy; a quarter-century later Nixonian detente signaled an attempt to *dis*establish ideology. To the degree that Nixon's attempt succeeded, it marked an end to the Cold War. What made the Cold War different from other phases of international relations was the ideology that infused the geopolitical struggle between the United States alliance system and the Soviet system. Empires, dynasties, and nation-states had vied for preeminence for as long as there had been such entities, but in most cases (though certainly not all cases: the Cold War was less unique than Americans — and Communist-orthodox Soviets — thought) the contenders had let power speak for itself and dispensed with universalistic belief systems that promised to transform humanity and end further struggle. The Cold War was a historical rarity: a geopolitical struggle in which both sides professed world-saving doctrines and insisted on sharing salvation with the rest of humanity.

The essence of detente was to divorce geopolitics from ideology. Nixon had never been the true-believing type, anyway; his long-standing anticommunism was sincere chiefly in the sense that he sincerely wanted to get ahead and sincerely believed that vitriolic denunciation of Communists and fellow travelers was the way to do it. But — as his actions while president demonstrated — power, not ideology, was what moved him. It was also what he believed moved others. To make the most of American power in the circumstances confronting the United States at the beginning of the 1970s, he had to jettison ideology: that is, to accept the Sino-Soviet split for the truly transforming event it was, and to exploit it by treating China and the Soviet Union as essentially ordinary great powers. Communists and capitalists would still have their disagreements, but these needn't preclude productive relations — any more than disagreements between Republicans and Democrats precluded productive relations between the two parties in the U.S. Congress.

Detente's immediate payoff was impressive. Nixon followed his China tour with a trip to Moscow, where he and Leonid Brezhnev inked the armistice that marked the formal end of the Cold War. A pair of arms-control agreements committed the superpowers to curtail the growth of their missile forces and to forgo comprehensive anti-missile defenses; less concrete but more indicative of detente's true meaning was a joint statement of twelve "basic principles" of U.S.-Soviet relations. Of these dozen the most important was the first, which asserted that despite differences in ideology, the superpowers would conduct their relations on the basis of "peaceful coexistence." Whatever their past disagreements, in the future the two governments would be guided by the principles of "sovereignty, equality, non-interference in internal affairs and mutual advantage."[5]

This was the big picture; a smaller piece of the puzzle, but one of great importance to Nixon, was the hoped-for effect of detente on Vietnam. If all went according to plan, the Soviets and the Chinese, eager for good relations with Washington more than with Hanoi, would cut back on aid to North Vietnam, thereby letting Vietnamization succeed. Over the longer term, detente would prevent further Vietnams: with American diplomacy liberated from the zero-sum thinking of the Cold War, the United States would no longer need to invest every small civil war with world-determining importance. Americans had indicated they wouldn't stand for any more Vietnams; Nixon made certain they wouldn't have to.

MISSION CREEP

To end the Cold War, Nixon relied on one of the central techniques of the Cold War: secrecy. To undermine Cold War liberalism,
he employed the same device. Yet while Nixon's termination of the
Cold War was deliberate, his sapping of liberalism was entirely in-
advertent, for in his own way he was as much a liberal as John
Kennedy or Lyndon Johnson. "I wanted to be an activist President
in domestic policy," he explained afterward. To be sure, he would be
a hard-headed activist, one who measured efficacy by outcome
rather than by intent. "I wanted to be certain that the things we did
had a chance of working. 'Don't promise to do more than we can do,'
I told the Cabinet. 'But do more than we can promise.'"[6]

As a Republican, Nixon naturally soft-pedaled his liberal tendencies. Indeed, he liked to characterize the centerpiece of his domestic
policy—the New Federalism—as a way of reversing decades of liberalism and returning control to the states and the people. In the
message unveiling his new approach, he called it "a turning point in
Federal-State relations, the beginning of decentralization of governmental power, the restoration of a rightful balance between the State
capitals and the national capital." In certain areas—education being
the most prominent—Nixon did in fact intend to return a certain
degree of control to the states. But the *federal* in New Federalism would remain crucial, for control over funding—and over the
taxing that would support the funding—would remain with Washington. Moreover, Nixon knew that the bureaucrats who had acquired power during the empire-building days of the 1960s would
be loath to relinquish it; in order to circumvent their obstruction-
ism, he would have to direct the devolution from the White House.
In other words (those of White House lawyer Leonard Garment),

"the central paradox of the Nixon administration was that in order to reduce *federal* power, it was first necessary to increase *presidential* power." (Although he appears not to have commented on it, Nixon must have seen the parallel in his domestic strategy to his Vietnam strategy of ending the war by intensifying it. Certainly both strategies appealed to his taste for deviousness.)[7]

Whatever he called his philosophy of governance, Nixon endorsed — and often initiated — a variety of policies associated with liberalism. He pushed the environmental ethic of the Rachel Carson school farther than Lyndon Johnson had dared. The Clean Air Act of 1970 was the most sweeping measure of its kind ever written; the Environmental Protection Agency, created the same year, became a bête noire of conservatives. To be sure, Nixon didn't give the forest-greens everything they wanted, which was why they regularly refused to credit his accomplishments. Or perhaps it was because they recognized that his environmentalism was a matter of the head, rather than of the heart. Nixon constantly weighed costs against benefits, and not infrequently found that the costs of doing the environmental right thing outweighed the benefits. "In a flat choice between smoke and jobs," he declared privately, "we're for jobs." Moreover, he could be a nasty partner. In a conversation with carmakers Henry Ford II and Lee Iacocca, Nixon warned that if the environmentalists had their way, Americans would have to "go back and live like a bunch of damned animals. . . . They're a group of people that aren't one really damn bit interested in safety or clean air. What they're interested in is destroying the system." Yet however ungracious he was, and however much his environmentalism was driven by political calculation, during Nixon's presidency environmentalists got more than during any presidency before or after.[8]

Nixon's record on race relations was similar. It was under Nixon that the promise of the *Brown* decision of 1954 was first seriously implemented across the South. As on the environment, on race Nixon was a grudging liberal. He made no grand gestures, like John Kennedy's telephone call to Martin Luther King in the Birmingham jail, and he uttered no stirring speeches on behalf of racial equality, like Lyndon Johnson's "We *shall* overcome" promise to Congress. Indeed, he gave enough hostages to the white South — by his "law and order" campaign of 1968, for example, and his nomination of Southerners Clement Haynsworth and G. Harrold Carswell for slots on the Supreme Court — that it was easy for his critics to contend that he was an obstacle to racial equality rather than an advocate of it. Yet as in his anti-environmentalist tirade to Ford and Iacocca, Nixon recognized the need to placate conservatives even as he undertook liberal reforms. When the Supreme Court decreed in 1969 that the two-track school systems that still characterized much of the South a decade and a half after *Brown* must be abolished forthwith, and black and white schools amalgamated, the president fielded a reporter's question as to what his policy would be now. "To carry out what the Supreme Court has laid down," he said. "I believe in carrying out the law even though I may have disagreed as I did in this instance with the decree that the Supreme Court eventually came down with. But we will carry out the law." By hiding behind the Court, Nixon could accomplish integration — which he recognized as inevitable — without alienating those white Southerners who were the key to the Republicans' emerging Sunbelt majority. At the same time, he understood that the best way to prevent integration from becoming a danger to the administration was to make sure it proceeded as smoothly and efficiently as possible. He put the prestige of the White House behind efforts to bring together black and white leaders of the South to devise local implementation plans, and he supplied federal money to facilitate the amalgamation of the dual school systems — and in fact asked for much more money than Congress proved willing to give.[9]

Nixon was also the first president to push affirmative action. His labor secretary, George Shultz, applied the "Philadelphia plan," which required contractors doing federal work to hire minimum numbers of black employees, to several cities across the country. In addition Nixon mandated the extension of affirmative action to women, enormously increasing the scope of the equal-results concept. To ensure enforcement of federal hiring guidelines, the administration requested, and received, dramatic increases in the staff and budget of the Equal Employment Opportunity Commission. In the same general area of workers' rights, Nixon sponsored the establishment of the Occupational Safety and Health Administration — an agency that soon would become synonymous, in conservative thinking, with bureaucratic busybodydom.

Even more infuriating to conservatives than OSHA was welfare. Republicans later liked to blame the big growth of welfare on the Great Society and its allegedly no-fault approach to family maintenance, but Nixon's approach was, if anything, more radical than Johnson's. In 1969 Nixon proposed a fundamental restructuring of the welfare system; his plan was to replace the several payments and services that constituted the nation's principal social safety net with a federal guaranteed income. As with some other of his initiatives, Nixon's "negative income tax" approach would diminish the power of the bureaucracy — in this case, those agencies that oversaw Aid to Families with Dependent Children, food stamps, Medicaid, school lunch programs, and the like — but would at the same time centralize authority, in the single office that administered the income policy. As a bonus, by reducing overhead it would allow the expansion of federal welfare coverage to millions more poor people, especially children.

Nixon's guaranteed income turned out to be too radical for Congress, although a less comprehensive version, embodied in the Supplemental Security Income program passed in 1972, effectively applied the concept to the elderly and infirm. And the adoption of uniform federal rules for food stamps greatly increased the coverage (and cost) of that grocery-buying program. Of equal lasting significance (and far greater long-term cost) was Nixon's decision to support automatic cost-of-living adjustments to Social Security payments. Although something less than a guaranteed income, the COLAs did guarantee that Social Security recipients would not lose ground relative to inflation (and in fact, if a large segment of a later generation of economists was correct, the COLAs actually guaranteed that recipients would *gain* ground, by overstating the real rise in the cost of living).

In all of this, there was more than a touch of Nixonian cynicism. The Tet offensive had shaken popular confidence in government but hardly shattered it, and the misgivings that were emerging had yet to cross over from the foreign side to the domestic. For a working majority of Americans, government still seemed the appropriate agent to tackle social problems. Nixon concurred, perhaps partly from conviction, probably partly because more power for government meant more power for *him,* and almost certainly because he hoped to keep the domestic reformers off his back so he could devote himself to foreign policy.

Had his presidency turned out differently, Nixon might have been accepted for the liberal he was — but for that to have happened, he would have had to change his entire approach to governing, if not his personality. Nixon found it constitutionally — both in the personal sense and referring to America's fundamental charter—impossible to approach his goals by open and direct methods. Perhaps he feared he lacked the rhetorical ability to attract voters to his views on various issues; considering his conspicuously off-putting speaking style, he was probably right. For whatever reasons, Nixon insisted on governing by stealth. His principal foreign policy initiatives were devised in secret and secretly set in motion; his domestic agenda was equally devious, if somewhat less covert.

The two sides of the president's penchant for secrecy were united—secretly of course—in the activities that gave rise to the Watergate scandal. Nixon embarked on his journey to the political underworld following publication by the *New York Times* of the Pentagon Papers. Some of Nixon's closest aides told him not to worry; this massive leak splashed mud on earlier administrations, not his own. "We have nothing to hide," said Chief of Staff H. R. Haldeman. "This is a family quarrel in the previous Administration regarding the Kennedy/Johnson conduct of the war. We, on the other hand, have developed a new policy and it's working."[10]

But of course Nixon *did* have something to hide, which was why he took the Pentagon Papers leak so seriously. At the time of publication, the White House was in the final stages of plotting the president's China *démarche extraordinaire;* the slightest slip could utterly ruin what had been years in the works. Meanwhile American negotiators were closeted with the Soviets in arms-control talks. A president didn't have to be paranoid to feel that a premature disclosure of Washington's bottom line might fatally undercut chances for a favorable deal.

For such reasons, Nixon ordered an embargo against the offending paper. "In view of the *New York Times'* irresponsibility and recklessness in deliberately printing classified documents without regard to the national interest," he told Haldeman, "I have decided that we must take action within the White House to deal with the problem. Until further notice under *no circumstances* is anyone connected with the White House to give any interview to a member of the staff of the *New York Times* without my express permission." The president added, in case Haldeman had somehow missed his drift: "I do not expect to give such permission in the foreseeable future."[11]

But the embargo failed. Hardly a month later, the *Times* did in fact disclose the administration's fallback position in the SALT talks, and the president was understandably outraged. He ordered his aides to find the sources of the leaks and plug them. The group that was gathered to carry out his orders — the Special Investigative Unit, colloquially the Plumbers — launched an investigation of Daniel Ellsberg, the former Pentagon official the Justice Department had charged with theft and unauthorized possession in the Pentagon Papers case. These were rather pedestrian charges, hardly the sort of thing to seriously deter other potential leakers — or, for that matter, Ellsberg himself, whom Nixon suspected of holding additional secrets. To strike a bit more terror into the souls of secret-tellers, the Plumbers surreptitiously raided the office of Ellsberg's psychiatrist. The goal was to obtain information that could be used either to fathom Ellsberg's future plans or to make a stronger judicial and political case against him.

In his enforced retirement, Nixon was unrepentant about the illegality of the raid. "I did not care about any reasons or excuses," he wrote. "I wanted someone to light a fire under the FBI in its investigation of Ellsberg. . . . I felt that his views had to be discredited. I urged that we find out everything we could about his background, his motives, and his co-conspirators, if they existed." Nixon claimed, not unbelievably, that he hadn't known about the break-in ahead of time. But he indicated, even more believably, if perhaps rather too circumspectly, that he wouldn't have prevented it if he *had* known. "I cannot say that had I been informed of it beforehand, I would have automatically considered it unprecedented, unwarranted, or unthinkable." Nixon conceded that with hindsight the break-in seemed wrong and excessive. "But I do not accept that it was as wrong or excessive as what Daniel Ellsberg did."

The Plumbers didn't get any good dirt at the psychiatrist's office, but neither did they get caught, and the administration was encouraged to broaden its investigations of those thought to be engaged in activities detrimental to national security. This cast the net widely, because Nixon increasingly came to see all those who opposed his foreign policies — particularly on Vietnam — as potential security threats. He admitted as much afterward, albeit in his characteristically exculpatory manner:

> In hindsight I can see that, once I realized the Vietnam war could not be ended quickly or easily and that I was going to be up against an antiwar movement that was able to dominate the media with its attitudes and values, I was sometimes drawn into the very frame of mind I so despised in the leaders of that movement. They increasingly came to justify almost anything in the name of forcing an immediate end to a war they considered unjustified and immoral. I was similarly driven to preserve the government's ability to conduct foreign policy and to conduct it in the way that I felt would best bring peace.[12]

As in every war America had fought, and as for years in the Cold War, so again in Nixon's administration: the line between foreign and domestic policy blurred and disappeared. Before long Nixon was defining nearly all his opponents as threats to national security.

It was this that preserved his conscience, such as it was, while the Plumbers and others associated with the administration and the Campaign to Re-elect the President broadened their covert political operations. The operations included wiretaps, mail openings, forged letters, further break-ins, and after the Watergate break-in that gave its name to the entire catalogue of capers, illicit efforts to obstruct investigations and keep the undercover work under cover. Twenty-five years earlier the American government had embarked on a campaign of covert operations against foreign enemies, or those believed to be enemies. It was one of the ironies of the Nixon administration that at the very moment when he was redefining the two countries that had been America's arch-enemies during the Cold War — the Soviet Union and China — as, if not quite friends, certainly something other than enemies, he was simultaneously discovering large numbers of enemies at home (one White House list counted more than two hundred, including such dangerous characters as pro football star Joe Namath and the leadership of the National Cleaning Contractors trade association) and employing covert techniques against them analogous to those that had been used against the villains abroad.

THE LAST HELICOPTER FROM THE SOUTH LAWN

The original purpose of the Plumbers was to protect the president's ability to conduct foreign policy; it was another irony of the time that the Plumbers and their collaborators wound up paralyzing Nixon in foreign policy. The Watergate scandal began surfacing at the most critical time for Nixon's policy in Vietnam: the months after the January 1973 accord that called a cease-fire and required the withdrawal of American troops from Vietnam. As long as American troops had remained on the ground in Vietnam, Nixon as commander-in-chief enjoyed a great deal of independence in the conduct of the war. The removal of the troops, by contrast, tilted the table toward Congress, which could now exercise its prerogatives as paymaster of foreign policy without having to worry about charges that it was leaving American boys defenseless before enemy fire. The legislature wasted little time; in August 1973 it ordered a halt to the bombing of Cambodia, and in November — just weeks after Nixon purged the Watergate prosecutor's office in the "Saturday night massacre" — it passed the War Powers Act, the most vigorous assertion of congressional control over the use of military force since 1787.

In Nixon's biased view, these actions sealed the fate of South Vietnam. "The congressional bombing cutoff," he wrote, "coupled with the limitation placed on the President by the War Powers Resolution in November 1973, set off a string of events that led to the Communist takeover in Cambodia and, on April 30, 1975, the North Vietnamese conquest of South Vietnam." There was something to Nixon's argument. For all the fine talk that surrounded the signing of the Paris accords, few people — even (or perhaps especially) among those turning all the fine phrases — really thought the Communists had abandoned their thirty-year quest for the reunification of Vietnam. The South Vietnamese government didn't think so, which was why President Nguyen Van Thieu tried to torpedo the cease-fire. The only hope of enforcing the settlement lay in the continued application of American power: bombs and military aid. By curtailing the bombing and, later, by cutting back funding for weapons for South Vietnam, congressional opponents of the war did indeed guarantee the failure of the Paris accords and the fall of South Vietnam.[13]

But in all likelihood they were simply guaranteeing the inevitable. The 1973 accord, by leaving the North Vietnamese troops in place in the South, was essentially indefensible. Saigon's soldiers had improved during the period of Vietnamization, but in terms of morale and resolve they were no match for their Communist counterparts, as the events of the spring of 1975 swiftly proved. The officer corps was riddled with corruption, rendering much of the American aid useless or worse.

Equally to the point, by assuming American support for the kind of enforcement the Paris accords required, Nixon was assuming far too much. Perhaps he thought his overwhelming victory in the 1972 election could be translated into support for his Vietnam policy. But the only thing that kept Americans really interested in South Vietnam was the American soldiers there and the American prisoners-of-war in North Vietnam. Even most Americans who had long backed the war effort were getting weary and wanted nothing more than to wash their country's hands of that endless conflict.

For all this, at the time of the signing of the accords there was a slim chance American voters would provide the necessary wherewithal to make enforcement at least a theoretical possibility. Nixon's actions in Watergate eliminated this slim chance. Even as Kissinger and Le Duc Tho were putting their pens to paper in Paris, the White House was placing pressure on the Watergate burglars, then on trial for the break-in, to keep quiet about their connections to the administration. The pressure finally failed, and the Watergate story began coming out. As it did, it destroyed the possibility that the United States would stand behind Nixon's promises to South Vietnam.

The imperatives of his foreign policy drove Nixon to Watergate; Watergate guaranteed the failure of that critical part of his foreign policy relating to Vietnam. Foreign policy and domestic politics had been entwined from the start of the Cold War; they remained entwined as the Cold War ended amid the ruins of America's Vietnam venture.

THE IMMOLATION OF THE LIBERALS

George Ball, on a journey to Pakistan during the Kennedy years, once asked President Ayub Khan why his country and the Indonesia of President Sukarno didn't collaborate in international affairs. "Pakistan is a nation of more than ninety million people; it is Islamic by constitution and non-Arab," Ball said. "There is only one other country in the world with similar characteristics, and that's Indonesia. It has a population of perhaps one hundred million people, is Islamic by constitution and non-Arab. I've often wondered why you don't make more common cause with the Indonesians."

Ayub looked carefully at the American undersecretary of state. "Do you really want to know, Mr. Secretary?" he asked. Ball said he did. "Well, the answer's very simple," the Pakistani president said. "Sukarno's such a shit."[14]

Liberals felt the same way about Nixon. Most of them had always been convinced that even if he occasionally did worthy things, he did them for the wrong reasons and therefore didn't deserve credit. Nixon returned the disdain and compounded it by the cynicism with which he pursued his political goals—including his own advancement. The fact that he won the presidency at a time when the Cold War paradigm was breaking down deepened the divide

between him and the liberals. He served a vital psychological purpose for liberals fleeing responsibility for Vietnam: by making the
war his, and by being such a devious and despicable character, he
provided a perfect scapegoat. Moreover, as the liberals bailed out on
Vietnam, many conveniently forgot that the Cold War — Vietnam's
progenitor and raison d'être — had originally been *their* idea. The
liberals, ignoring that Nixon was in the process of liquidating the
Cold War, recalled his early contributions to the Cold War and felt
further reassured by their apparent distance from him.

For all these reasons, liberals delighted in Nixon's Watergate discomfiture. They cheered each damning discovery by the Watergate
prosecutor and each tawdry revelation before the Senate Watergate
committee. They applauded the posse that pursued Nixon up the
hill of executive privilege and down the dale of illegal campaign
contributions. They whooped when the fugitive was cornered at
San Clemente and cheered when he was brought to ground for his
crimes by the Supreme Court and the House Judiciary Committee.

So swept up in the spirit of the times were they that they added
their own indictments, and not just of Nixon but of presidents prior
to Tricky Dick. Senate investigators traced covert operations back
to the early years of the Cold War. They laid bare the CIA plots
against the governments of Guatemala and Iran during the 1950s
and against the lives of Cuba's Castro and the Congo's Patrice
Lumumba in the early 1960s. They caught the FBI eavesdropping on
leftists and smearing civil rights leaders as Communists.

Having consigned the Cold War to someone else's history, most
liberals felt righteously indignant at all the dirty laundry. (A few,
preferring the confessional mode, acknowledged a collective com-
plicity before assuring voters that salvation had since arrived.) They
wrung their hands and clucked their tongues; they passed measures

to corral the "rogue elephant" the CIA was said to be, and to restrain the "imperial presidency" allegedly responsible for such excess. All this was understandable — a natural response to a traumatic war gone bad, an arrogant presidency run amok, and a generation of foreign policy busted.

It was also fatal to the liberal enterprise. Every revelation of dirty dealing, cynical manipulation, and calculated deception by Nixon, Johnson, Kennedy, Eisenhower, and Truman exacerbated the distrust of government that Vietnam had engendered. Briefly it had been possible to believe that Watergate was something peculiar to this latest administration, and in its exaggerated form it was. But every week new evidence revealed that the American government had been shading the truth since the first years of the Cold War. At a certain level, Americans had always understood this — at least well enough not to ask too many questions. As long as the Cold War had delivered the goods, they were willing to suspend their skepticism and follow Washington's lead. Partly because trust tends to extrapolate — if government could be trusted on apocalyptic issues like war and peace in the nuclear age, it ought to be able to handle lunches for school kids and health care for old folks — and partly because most matters of domestic politics got swept into the discourse of the Cold War, the era of the Cold War consensus became the halcyon period for domestic liberalism. But when the Cold War cracked up in Vietnam, it shattered the consensus, ravaged popular faith in government, and scorched the earth from which the liberal agenda had sprung. The liberals, by disowning the Cold War and contributing to its disgrace, seared the earth that much more, and ensured a long season of fallow.

6

THE CONTRADICTIONS OF COLD WAR CONSERVATISM

The demise of liberalism in the mid-1970s left the field of American politics in confusion. Jimmy Carter was elected in 1976 as neither a liberal nor a conservative but an outsider; his four years in office accomplished little beyond allowing conservatives time to regroup. They needed it, for they had been wandering in the wilderness so long that they hardly knew what conservatism meant any more. New varieties of conservatism, largely unrecognizable to pre-Cold War conservatives, sprang up. Of these the noisiest and most pretentious was neoconservatism, a hybrid ideology that afforded a haven for refugee intellectuals of the old Left of the 1930s who now denounced socialism as fervently as they had once embraced it. The neoconservatives, activists by temperament, advocated a decidedly unconservative activism against the Soviet Union. They asserted that the Cold War was not over, that the struggle initially joined by the first generation of Cold War liberals — men like Harry Truman, who suddenly became a darling of the Right — continued, and must continue.

Ronald Reagan, himself a lapsed liberal, adopted most of the neoconservative message, albeit instinctively rather than intellectually. If he had been more of an intellectual, or simply more thoughtful, he might have been bothered by the inconsistency between his philosophy of domestic affairs, which posited that government was the central problem of American society and the source of most avoidable evil, and his approach to foreign affairs, which asked Americans to trust their government to wage a renewed Cold War by the means that had so recently been discredited.

American voters proved to be more consistent than Reagan. They accepted his anti-government message in domestic affairs, endorsing the first serious rollback of federal authority since the 1920s. But they rejected his call for a renewed anti-Communist crusade. For them, Cold War II consisted chiefly of a weapons buildup, which had immediate payoffs in terms of profits and jobs. As for the contra war in Central America, the armed intervention in Lebanon, and various other suggestions of an activist foreign policy, Americans registered little but apathy, skepticism, and scorn.

WHY *NOT* THE BEST?

The disintegration of liberalism made a swing to conservatism inevitable, but not immediate. Mostly because conservatives had forgotten what they stood for, there weren't any credible conservative candidates in the mid-1970s. Indeed, the first post-Watergate, post-Nixon election filled the House with Democrats, many of whom retained the liberal tendencies of their party.

But Vietnam had riven the party of Jefferson and Jackson as deeply as Watergate wounded Lincoln's. The riot that passed for a Democratic national convention in 1968, followed by Hubert

Humphrey's half-point defeat in the general election, had demoralized Democratic regulars, who were still nursing their grudges when the refugees of Grant Park linked arms with other outsider factions in the summer of 1970 to rewrite the rules governing selection of delegates to subsequent conventions. The first such convention took place in 1972, and the delegates certainly did represent a broader slice of American demography than previous conventions. Women, blacks, and Chicanos were better represented than ever in American history, and in their opposition to the status quo they determined to nominate a candidate similarly opposed.

The ironic thing was that they wound up with a man who, except for a single issue, could hardly have been more mainstream. George McGovern was a preacher's son from the heartland, a decorated war veteran, a career politician who until 1965 had dedicated himself chiefly to public works and parity for South Dakota's farmers. He was also a thoroughly decent fellow: patient, tolerant, and devoted to the national welfare. Until 1965 his highest ambition had been to head the Department of Agriculture.

But the escalation of the war in Vietnam — especially the bombing, which, with his air corps background, he understood better than most civilian officials in the Johnson administration — offended his sense of morality and patriotism. He began speaking out against the war, although in measured tones that gave the Johnson administration credit for good faith if not good judgment. With nearly every other political pro in America, he reckoned that an open break with the president would be political folly — quixotically fatal to himself, ultimately futile for the country. Better to bore from within, pushing the party gradually toward peace.

Events of the spring of 1968 changed his mind, as they changed the minds of so many others. Eugene McCarthy's New Hampshire challenge showed Johnson to be beatable, causing McGovern to consider a run of his own. But Robert Kennedy got there first, and rather than splinter the antiwar movement further, McGovern fell in line behind the former attorney general. Only after Kennedy's June assassination did McGovern determine to make a race—by which time the juggernaut of Vice President Hubert Humphrey had gained unstoppable momentum. McGovern played the good soldier and backed Humphrey—an easy choice, considering the opposition.

McGovern began preparing another race almost before Humphrey lost to Nixon. That the war continued into 1972 increased his determination even as it enhanced his credibility. Unfortunately, it also tended to narrow his political base. The war became the single issue on which he focused—not least because it was about the only issue on which the diverse factions that now dominated the party's nominating system could agree. He carried the convention without great difficulty but discovered that indignation about the war wasn't nearly enough to carry the general election. The draw-down of American troops in Vietnam was almost complete, and Henry Kissinger was making sufficient progress at the peace talks in Paris to be able to declare, more or less convincingly, that peace was at hand. Meanwhile Watergate remained covered up. The McGovern campaign compounded its difficulties by a variety of amateurish mistakes, of which the most damaging was its failure to fully investigate the background of McGovern's running-mate, Thomas Eagleton. When reporters discovered that Eagleton had undergone electroshock treatment for a mental condition some years earlier, McGovern felt obliged to dump him in favor of Sargent Shriver.

By this time, the liberals were in full flight from responsibility for Vietnam, and although Nixon's position on many domestic issues wasn't that much different from McGovern's, the South Dakota senator became the symbol of liberalism. As a result, liberalism became freighted with much of McGovern's baggage, and he got tagged as the candidate of the "triple A: acid, amnesty, and abortion" — for the presence in the campaign of former hippie types, for his antiwar views and sympathy with war resisters, and for his pro-choice position on abortion. When he proposed a peace dividend of a thousand dollars in cash for every person in America, liberalism as a movement came to appear hopelessly muddled and naive. And after he lost to Nixon in the worst electoral disaster in modern American history, liberalism came to appear just plain hopeless.

The McGovern debacle threw the Democrats into utter confusion; Watergate shortly thereafter did the same to the Republicans. Between them, these two events primed the country for the candidacy of Jimmy Carter, an outsider who wore his conscience on his sleeve (he confessed — in *Playboy* magazine, of all places — to have "looked on a lot of women with lust. I've committed adultery in my heart many times") but concealed his ambition behind his aw-shucks Georgia smile. Carter toured the country for three years preparing the ground for his presidential race; he pounded home the message that America needed a government as good as its people.[1]

After all they had gone through during the previous decade, American voters were willing to give the candidate who had been farthest from the scene of the crimes of Vietnam and Watergate the greatest benefit of the doubt. Incumbent Gerald Ford would have run a better race if he hadn't tarred himself with the Watergate brush by pardoning Nixon just a month after Nixon's resignation; as it was, the 1976 contest was hardly a Democratic runaway, suggesting that the 1974 Democratic sweep represented a vote *against* Watergate rather than *for* the Democratic party.

Carter's victory was equally a protest against incumbency. Voters couldn't really know what they were getting in this new fellow, who had been tactically, but also philosophically, ambiguous during the campaign. "I was a fiscal conservative but quite liberal on such issues as civil rights, environmental quality, and helping people overcome handicaps to lead fruitful lives," he explained afterward. Linking himself to Southern populists of an earlier era, he elaborated, "Among the most important goals in the Southern brand of populism was to help the poor and aged, to improve education, and to provide jobs. At the same time the populists tried not to waste money, having almost an obsession about the burden of excessive debt."[2]

As chief executive, Carter quickly gained a reputation for micromanagement — for attending personally to the myriad details required to make an administration run. But amid his obsession for specifics, a pattern emerged in which four areas of presidential interest stood out: energy, education, welfare, and urban affairs. His energy program was designed to reduce American dependence on foreign oil, a pressing problem since the Arab oil embargo of 1973–74. But, as was evident from the moment he unveiled his energy policy in February 1977, he couldn't decide whether to marshal the power of government against energy spendthrifts or simply to rely on suasion and executive example. In the latter direction, he labeled the energy crisis the "moral equivalent of war," urged Americans to carpool and lower their thermostats, and offered the conservation-cum-style statement of cardigan sweaters worn before cozy fires. In the more coercive vein, he called for higher taxes on oil and natural gas; a new Department of Energy would enforce the administration's policy.[3]

Carter's other reform proposals were as much organizational as substantive. A new Department of Education, to be spun off from Health, Education, and Welfare (HEW), would coordinate federal activities in support of the nation's schools. His welfare package consisted chiefly of measures to eliminate duplication among the several cash, in-kind, and services programs. The cities would benefit from better management of existing resources; small amounts of fresh money would deliver maximum impact through federal-state and public-private teamwork.

Coming from a professed populist, this was a remarkably modest agenda, and the results Carter achieved in pursuit of his agenda were more modest still. The Department of Energy did come into being, but the rest of the president's energy policy (except for the sweaters on White House staffers) foundered on resistance from the oil industry and motorists. When the second "oil shock," the one that accompanied the fall of the Shah of Iran, sent oil prices — and petro-profits — to levels that were commonly labeled obscene, Carter won a windfall-profits tax from Congress. But shortly thereafter he suffered the almost unheard-of ignominy of having a veto — in this case, of a bill that failed to include a new tax on oil imports — overridden by a Congress controlled by his own party. The outcome of his education, welfare, and urban initiatives — such as they were — was less embarrassing but hardly more gratifying. He got his Department of Education, but that department got little more than it had in HEW; welfare and urban reform were mugged by illiberal lobbies and picked apart by contending congressional committees.

The fate of Carter's domestic program offered scant guidance as to the direction of American politics. Because it was neither particularly liberal nor clearly conservative to begin with, its overall failure was a philosophical wash. Liberals could find little to cheer in the Georgia president's performance, but conservatives could find little more.

BETWEEN IRAQ AND A HARD PLACE

The ambivalence of the Carter years was even more marked in foreign policy. The Democratic president virtually ignored the fact that Gerald Ford was his immediate predecessor; Nixon's was the ghost he wrestled. "Our first movie in the White House was *All the President's Men*," he recorded in his diary two days after inauguration. "I felt strange occupying the same living quarters and position of responsibility as Richard Nixon."[4]

Along with the house and responsibilities, Carter inherited a foreign policy — in particular, the post-Cold War policy of detente — that left him feeling equally strange. On one hand, having got past the Cold War afforded some relief. The United States, he explained in an early speech, was now "free of that inordinate fear of communism" which for years had caused Americans to sacrifice their higher impulses to the struggle with the Soviets. "I'm glad that's being changed." On the other hand, for both political and temperamental reasons Carter had grave problems with the geopolitical pragmatism that underpinned detente — at least as designed by Nixon and Kissinger. In poor light, pragmatism can be confused with cynicism, and the light of the post-Watergate era was worse than ever. Carter had to distance himself from Nixon in this regard, as in so many others. He had almost no choice but to appeal to American idealism, in foreign policy as in domestic. Necessity wasn't especially onerous here, for as in the domestic realm, the appeal to the higher virtues reflected the new president's personality.

When Cold War presidents had been feeling moral, they generally harped on the perfidy of the Communists and the comparative (or, occasionally, absolute) moral elevation of the Free World. Unless he wanted to disown detente and try to revive the Cold War, this wasn't an option for Carter, who instead hit upon human rights as an appropriate outlet for American idealism, and his own. He insisted that a commitment to human rights must serve as a centerpiece of American foreign policy — as, lamentably, it had not during the Cold War. "For too many years, we've been willing to adopt the flawed and erroneous principles and tactics of our adversaries," he said, "sometimes abandoning our own values for theirs. We've fought fire with fire, never thinking that fire is better quenched with water." It was time to bring out the hoses. "The great democracies are not free because we are strong and prosperous. We are strong and influential and prosperous because we are free." Americans must share this insight with the world. "Our policy is rooted in our moral values. Our policy is designed to serve mankind."[5]

Liberals applauded Carter's priorities. In their post-Vietnam amnesia, most liberals believed that Carter's policies were precisely the sort liberals had always advocated. To some degree this was true — although during the Cold War there had frequently been a large gap between advocacy and practice, which was precisely the point Carter was making. Where the ideological rubber hit the geopolitical road, the Cold War liberals had quite often been willing to set aside liberality and focus on results. What Carter was saying was that the interventionism of the Cold War was a thing of the past. Or if there must be intervention, it would be of a moral sort, enforced not by tanks and planes but by American disapproval of miscreants.

If many liberals didn't have a clear view of what Carter was attempting, the neoconservatives did — and they recoiled at what they saw. They had liked the Cold War, and they liked it even more now that it was sliding into nostalgia. They excoriated Carter for "isolationism" (sometimes "neo-isolationism," presumably in keeping with their own neo-status) and leveled against the administration the all-purpose epithet of the post-Munich era: "appeasement." Determined to resurrect the Cold War, they set about destroying Carter.

During the first two years of Carter's term, their efforts came to little. The president succeeded in negotiating and then ratifying a new set of Panama Canal treaties, despite the objections of neoconservatives (and some others) that he was selling out a vital American interest. He cajoled, shamed, and bribed the governments of Egypt and Israel into signing a peace treaty ending the thirty-year state of war between those Middle East antagonists. He won Soviet acceptance of the SALT II treaty, which for the first time would actually reduce the number of intercontinental missiles.

But he never got the Senate to ratify the SALT II accord, for events of the last eighteen months of his term gave the neoconservatives the opening they needed to drive a stake through the heart of detente. The Nicaraguan revolution suggested that communism was on the march once more (the neocons argued that it had never stopped marching but that Americans had deliberately closed their ears to the sound of the tramping feet). The Iranian revolution was harder to link to the international Left, given that Ayatollah Khomeini and his followers had even less use for the atheistic adherents of Marx and Lenin than for the capitalist cadres of Adam Smith. But the neocons nonetheless cited the overthrow of the Shah, a longtime American ally (if at times a rather obstreperous one), as evidence of what the self-abnegation of detente inevitably led to. When Iranian students stormed the American embassy in Teheran in November 1979 and seized six dozen American hostages, the neoconservatives acidly asked why it was that the Iranian radicals had picked on the American embassy, rather than the Soviet. The answer, they said, was clear: the radicals feared and respected Russia, but not the United States.

As well they might have — or so it seemed two months later, when the Soviet Union launched a major military operation against Afghanistan. Islamic rebels in that country were threatening to topple the government, a development the Kremlin, as the uneasy master of the scores of millions of Muslims in the Soviet republics of Central Asia, could view only with alarm.

The Kremlin's alarm, and the invasion it triggered, set the klaxons blaring in neoconservative circles. On scant evidence, neoconservative scaremongers asserted that the thrust into Afghanistan portended a Catherine-the-Great-style sweep down through discombobulated Iran to the warm waters and oil fields of the Persian Gulf. To such dire straits — including the Strait of Hormuz — did detente ineluctably lead.

The Soviet invasion of Afghanistan — coming while the American hostages still languished in Teheran — knocked the props from under Carter's foreign policy. Although detente had never depended on Soviet amiability, critics could easily portray it so, and enough of the zero-sum mindset of the Cold War persisted that many Americans were willing to believe that a gain for radical forces anywhere represented a setback for the United States. Carter didn't help his case by conceding, shortly after the Soviets entered Afghanistan, that "my opinion of the Russians has changed more drastically in the last week than in the two and one-half years before that." Such an admission hardly inspired confidence.[6]

SAINT RON AND THE DRAGON

Confidence was the critical question, as it had been for forty years. Carter's approval rating plummeted during the first several months of 1980; by the dog days of summer Carter was deeper in the doghouse than any president since Gallup started tracking such things. Politicians erect psychological defenses to explain away popular distaste for themselves and their policies, but Carter must have had to work extra hard to rationalize the fact that his 21 percent approval rating was three points below Richard Nixon's on the eve of resignation.[7]

As they almost always do, domestic issues counted for more in the election of 1980 than foreign affairs, and in choosing Ronald Reagan, voters had more to criticize about the condition of the economy than about the state of the world. Needless to say, the national embarrassment that accompanied the continuing captivity of the hostages in Iran didn't improve voters' opinion of Carter, but the double whammy of inflation and unemployment hit much closer to home for many who pulled the lever for the Republican non-incumbent. Four years earlier, Carter had used the phrase "misery index" against Gerald Ford; now he found himself at the business end of this sum of the inflation and jobless figures.

Reagan understood the critical role of confidence; at times his campaign, and subsequently his presidency, sounded like a commercial for a course in the power of positive thinking. Public optimism had been his stock-in-trade since his days as spokesman for General Electric, whose primary product, he and other GE flacks liked to say, was progress. Reagan was an actor, but he was a character actor, and as with many character actors, his performance mirrored his persona. Reagan's optimism, according to journalist Lou Cannon, who made a California-to-Washington career of observing the governor-turned-president, was "not a trivial or peripheral quality. It was the essential ingredient of an approach to life that had carried Reagan from the backwaters of Dixon [Illinois] to fame as a sports announcer and then to the stages of Hollywood and of the world." Reagan's slogan as a candidate was "Let's make America great again"; as president he described a country "standing tall" and urged Americans to "dream heroic dreams"; his reelection campaign in 1984 asserted that it was "morning again in America."[8]

Yet there was a curious discontinuity in Reagan's message. The country was as great as ever, he said, but its government was awful. "Government is not the solution to our problem," he stated in his first inaugural. "Government *is* the problem." How a government elected by the American people could be so bad, he didn't explain. It wasn't the voters' fault: Reagan never stopped praising the American people. It wasn't a problem with democracy per se: popular rule was one of the crowning gems of national glory, and it was what had inspired Lincoln, in words Reagan repeated over and over, to call America "the last best hope of man on earth." It wasn't *his* fault: he was doing his best to undo the damage government had wrought. It wasn't the Republican party's fault: his party had joined with him in this noble effort. It must be the Democrats' fault—even though every one of those Democrats had been selected for office by those wonderful American voters, acting through the inestimable institutions of democracy.[9]

Consistency, however, has rarely been a requisite for political success in America, and the American people registered real enthusiasm for Reagan's anti-government message. Events of the Vietnam-Watergate era had destroyed public faith in government, resetting the clock of popular confidence to some time in the era of Grant or Harding—in any case, to the pre-Cold War era when skepticism toward government, rather than trust, characterized the national psyche. Reagan made the most of this skepticism, assailing government at every turn and taking a pickax to every program he could reach.

Every program but defense, that is. If Reagan's attitude toward government—the government *he* headed—was somewhat paradoxical, his attitude toward foreign affairs was downright contradictory. Even as he declared that government could do no right, that government bureaucrats were untrustworthy or otherwise inept, he called on the American people to fall into step behind their government and support the policies devised by government bureaucrats in a new crusade against communism.

And it was a crusade, indeed, that Reagan called for. Not since the earliest years of the Cold War had American policy assumed such overtly moralistic form. In his first press conference as president, Reagan declared that the goal of the present leadership of the Soviet Union was what the Communists' goal had always been: "world revolution and a one-world Socialist or Communist state, whichever word you want to use." He added that "the only morality they recognize is what will further their cause, meaning they reserve unto themselves the right to commit any crime, to lie, to cheat, in order to attain that." Subsequently he described the Soviet Union as "the focus of evil in the modern world" and — his most memorable phrase — "an evil empire." In the address containing this last characterization, he minced no words in describing the contest between America and Russia as a "struggle between right and wrong and good and evil." The real crisis in international affairs, he said, was "a test of moral will and faith." At every opportunity, with studied earnestness, Reagan intoned "God bless America" in a voice suggesting a reasonable certainty the Deity would do just that.[10]

Reagan's moralism appears to have been informed by a semiliteral belief in the prophecies of Armageddon — prophecies that were quite influential among the Christian Right that constituted one of his core constituencies. Reagan, an inveterate storyteller and a sporadic (if that) churchgoer, was entranced by the drama of the Bible, of which no book is more dramatic than Revelations. With many Biblical literalists, Reagan read the founding of Israel in 1948 as a critical step on the path to the final, climactic contest between good and evil. "For the first time ever," he offered in 1971, "everything is in place for the battle of Armageddon and the second coming of Christ." In 1980 he told a television interviewer, "We may be the generation that sees Armageddon."[11]

Reagan downplayed the Armageddon theme after winning the presidency, not least because his handlers realized it made people nervous. Would a president who believed Armageddon nigh, and who also controlled more than twenty thousand nuclear weapons, be tempted to weigh in with those weapons on the side of the Lord? Yet Reagan certainly wasn't reluctant about casting America's lot with the forces of good (as he saw them) in the smaller contests that marked the shifting boundary between Soviet influence and American. With the neoconservatives — many of whom staffed his foreign-policy team — Reagan believed that the Cold War had never ended, only American participation in that ongoing struggle for the world. Detente, he declared, was "a one-way street that the Soviet Union has used to pursue its own aims." This one-way street had led to the entrenchment of radicalism in Angola, in the Horn of Africa, in Central America, in Afghanistan, in Indochina — not to mention communism's preexisting hold on the Soviet Union, Eastern Europe, and China. For ten years, since the inception of detente, the Free World had been losing ground. If freedom were to survive, it needed to mount a counteroffensive, and soon.[12]

The problem was that Americans, by and large, weren't interested. Besides those many who got jittery at the loose talk of nuclear war — loose talk that included an abysmally poor joke by the president about bombing Moscow — many more Americans had a hard time getting worked up about the fate of such countries as Angola, Somalia, Nicaragua, and Cambodia. In an earlier era, Americans had been willing to accept Truman's warning that the survival of liberty depended on the right side winning in Greece and Turkey and South Korea, and the predictions of Truman and Eisenhower and Kennedy and Johnson and Nixon that a Communist victory in Vietnam would jeopardize the peace of the world, and those same presidents' assurances that American alliances with and American aid to dozens of countries around the world were all that finally stood between freedom and tyranny. None of these statements had been proved right, partly because negatives are impossible to prove in history. Had the Soviets refrained from attacking West Germany because of the American troops stationed there, or had the Kremlin never had any intention of attacking? And at least one of the statements had been proven egregiously wrong: Vietnam went communist, but Southeast Asia was more capitalist than ever. Even China had started down the capitalist road, if not the democratic road.

The problem wasn't simply Vietnam, and it wasn't simply history. Reagan had made a career of blaming government for the failings of American society. He continued to do so, even now that he sat at the head of the national government. He did his work well — too well for the kind of activist foreign policy he envisioned. Americans who listened to their president constantly bash government were hardly inclined to trust that same government to conduct a foreign policy whose connection to vital American interests had to be taken on faith — that is, faith in the judgment of those allegedly incompetent government officials. Reagan repeatedly advocated American support of "freedom fighters" around the world — rebels contesting Left-leaning, and often Soviet-backed, regimes. The most prominent of the good-guy guerrilla groups, in Reaganite rhetoric and thinking, was the "contra" army in Nicaragua. For three years the administration channeled funds to the contras, and the CIA, under unreconstructed Cold Warrior William Casey, supplied advice, training, and sundry other support.

But the American people never warmed to the contras. At the beginning of 1984, Gallup asked Americans what they thought of the administration's Central American policy; respondents decisively turned thumbs down. Those who disapproved of the policy outnumbered those who approved by a margin of 49 percent to 28 percent. And this was *before* word got out that the CIA had planted mines in the harbor waters of Nicaragua, in clear violation of international law. The mine-laying scheme brought back memories of the agency's bad old days, and provoked the Senate to condemn the action by the overwhelming margin of eighty-four to twelve.

On the whole, voters found little to like in the president's foreign policy. A recent intervention in Lebanon, which had resulted in the bombing deaths of more than 250 Americans, was even less popular than the Central American campaign. The same poll that returned the heavy disapproval for the contra war rejected the administration's actions in Lebanon by more than two to one (59 percent disapproving against 28 percent approving). After three years of effort by the administration to generate enthusiasm for an activist foreign policy, voters found foreign policy to be distinctly the weakest aspect of the administration's program. In January 1984, only 38 percent of voters registered approval of the administration's overall foreign policy, while 49 percent disapproved.[13]

THE FORCE BE WITH YOU

The one area in which Americans registered any substantial support for Reagan's effort to revive the Cold War — and then only briefly — was military rearmament. The neoconservatives had long excoriated arms control as controlling American arms but not Russian. There was enough to this argument for it to be plausible: by counting launchers rather than throw weight, the SALT system allowed the Soviets to retain the monster missiles that gave them an edge in land-based megatonnage. That the United States had deliberately decided to concentrate on precision rather than magnitude was lost on the SALT–busters, who delighted in publishing pictorial comparisons of the arsenals of the two sides, with giant missiles marked with the hammer and sickle overshadowing pipsqueaks bearing the Stars and Stripes. The neoconservatives spoke ominously of a "window of vulnerability": a period commencing soon during which Moscow would be able to conduct a disarming first strike against America's nuclear forces, leaving the United States to capitulate or lose its cities and most of its population.

This dire scenario had serious logical and psychological problems. Were the Soviet missiles as accurate as the neocons claimed? Could the Kremlin rely on an American president accepting several million dead without retaliating? What about America's submarine-based missiles, which remained invulnerable? But in the atmosphere of alarm that surrounded the revolutions in Nicaragua and Iran and the invasion of Afghanistan, the neoconservatives gained a hearing denied to them since the onset of detente. Jimmy Carter caved during his final year in office, requesting a sizable increase in defense spending, the first since the Vietnam war.

This was only the beginning. Reagan entered office vowing to restore American prestige and credibility; the imagery of "standing tall" included a massive arms buildup to replace those puny missiles with bigger brothers that would match anything the Russians had. Between 1981 and 1985, American spending on defense leaped a third, from $179 billion in fiscal 1981 to $229 billion in 1985 (in constant 1982 dollars). Every military service received major infusions of cash and firepower: the army, new tanks and rockets and troop carriers; the navy, the keels for a six-hundred-ship fleet; the air force, the latest in stealth and missile technology; the marines, the most powerful ground-support aircraft.[14]

The pièce de résistance of the Reagan buildup was unveiled in 1983. The president, like many conservatives (and more than a few others), had never reconciled himself to the strategy of nuclear deterrence. He refused to accept that America's continued survival depended on something as flimsy as the rationality of the headmen of communism (whose rationality was suspect on the very account of their adherence to that wrong-headed doctrine); in one of his few areas of agreement with certain elements of the Left, he thought the doctrine of Mutual Assured Destruction was precisely what the acronym spelled. To remedy the situation, and to restore American security to American control, he introduced his Strategic Defense Initiative (SDI), a space-based system of anti-missile defense. Immediately dubbed Star Wars, this system would neutralize the Soviet threat by enabling the United States to shoot down incoming Soviet missiles.

Critics assailed Star Wars for violating the Anti-ballistic Missile Treaty of 1972 (praised by SDI opponents as the single most successful arms-control measure of the nuclear age), for destabilizing deterrence (in that the imminent neutralization of their arsenal might provoke the Russians to attack before the new system came on line), for being unachievable (the necessary technologies were many years away, and in any event the Russians could counter improvements in U.S. defenses by simply increasing their offensive capability), and for breaking the budget (at a time of already historic deficits).

After the fact, the Reaganites took this last complaint and converted it into the most important recommendation of SDI. The very expense of having to match the United States in this new, and unprecedentedly expensive, leg of the arms race, they said, was what caused the Kremlin to cry Uncle Sam and abandon its pretensions to superpower status. The argument received just enough support from the morning-after testimony of Soviet leaders to be plausible, but not enough to silence skeptics on the subject, and in any event, like most arguments about causation in history, it was undisprovable.

WHOSE OXYMORON IS BEING GORED?

Whatever its effect on Soviet thinking, the Reagan arms buildup had a decided effect on the American economy. The weapons industry felt the effect first and most directly. The industry had been slumping since the winding down of the Vietnam war, but the first half of the 1980s brought an abrupt reversal. Profit margins in Standard & Poor's aerospace/defense sector averaged almost 50 percent higher in 1985 than a decade before (9.6 percent against 6.8 percent); dollar earnings per share, which had hovered in the single digits during the mid-1970s, vaulted into the twenties and thirties during the Reagan years.[15]

The effect on the economy as a whole was less dramatic but no less significant. Even while the Reaganites ridiculed Keynesianism as liberal looniness, they practiced the Keynesian formula of deficit spending. Tax cuts enacted in the name of supply-side economics (whose central argument was that reductions in tax rates would spur economic growth sufficient to pay for the tax cuts and then some), in conjunction with the big increase in military spending and the natural growth of non-discretionary spending (spending required by previous legislation), sent the federal deficit to levels inconceivable just a few years before.

Nearly everyone — Republicans and Democrats, liberals and conservatives — shook their heads at the runaway deficits. Democrats blamed Republicans for bloating defense and coddling capital; Republicans blamed Democrats for winking at wasteful social programs. But neither side took the drastic measures necessary to erase the deficits, for fear of alienating important constituencies and bursting the bubble of economic recovery. After a sharp but brief recession during Reagan's first two years, the economy entered a long phase of steady growth — just as the Keynesian model predicted. The Reagan administration disputed the Keynesian connection — the tax cuts simply unleashed the entrepreneurial energies of the American people, administration supporters said — but the president and his partisans were happy to take credit for the bounty of the times.

If the deficits weren't quite what conservatism had traditionally called for, in other respects the Reagan years were the most conservative since Herbert Hoover. The president signaled hostility to organized labor when in 1981 he fired more than ten thousand members of the air-traffic-controllers' union for striking the Federal Aviation Administration — even though the union in question had been one of the few to support his candidacy in 1980. His tax cuts reversed the progressive principle that had been built into the tax codes over the years; individuals in the highest brackets received the largest cuts, with the top rate tumbling by more than half, from 70 percent to 33 percent (it later crept back up slightly).

The story was similar on the spending side. Although programs that had come to be considered entitlements by the politically potent middle class — Social Security and Medicare, to name the most obvious — largely resisted downsizing, programs designed to help the poor were more vulnerable. School lunches were slashed (with the administration notoriously redefining ketchup as a vegetable and adopting other dietary devices to trim costs while preserving appearances). Mass transit lost funding, forcing many of those without cars to walk or simply stay home. They discovered they had less reason to get out when job-training programs were terminated.

Reaganites defended such reductions as necessary to eliminate the abuses inflicted on honest taxpayers by the likes of the "welfare queens" who had long been a staple of anti-liberal demonology; at the same time, such cuts were part of a larger effort to diminish the scope of government in American life. Deregulation — commenced by Carter in the transportation industry — was extended to other areas of the economy, most notably investment and finance. The 1980s witnessed an orgy of corporate takeovers, friendly and hostile; mergers heretofore prevented by the Justice Department's antitrust squad — or by fear of the same — now were consummated with an abandon that shocked even many defenders of Wall Street's wisdom and virtue. The savings-and-loan industry experienced an outbreak of the Las Vegas syndrome: as lenders flipped real estate and pyramided debt, some made vast fortunes while others lost everything. (When the pyramid collapsed during the late 1980s, the government had to step back in and pick up the pieces.)

Deregulation demonstrated the conservative faith of the administration, in the opinion of some observers, but for others the decidedly unconservative deficits counted for more. A disillusioned David Stockman, after bailing out as White House budget director, declared of his old bailiwick: "By 1984 it had become a dreamland. It was holding the American economy hostage to a reckless, unstable fiscal policy based on the politics of high spending and the doctrine of low taxes." But whatever the economic inconsistencies, the formula was political magic, and the president was reelected overwhelmingly in that same dreamy year.[16]

Reagan's foreign-policy inconsistencies did him hardly more damage. Early in his second term, the president was caught out in a position that would have destroyed other administrations. In June 1985, after a year in which scores of Americans had been kidnapped in the Middle East by factions partial to Iran, thirty-nine of the hostages were released. Rumors immediately surfaced of a deal between Washington and Teheran. Reagan issued an indignant denial. "The United States gives terrorists no rewards and no guarantees," he declared. "We make no concessions. We make no deals." But administration actions belied the president's words. The White House was orchestrating secret deliveries of weapons to Iran, then engaged in a struggle to the death with Iraq; the objective of the deliveries was the release of the remaining hostages.[17]

More precisely, the release of the hostages was the *primary* objective of the secret Iranian arms deals; a secondary purpose was the generation of funds to support the Nicaraguan contras. The apathy of American voters toward Reagan's Central American adventure evolved into antipathy, and in 1984 Congress passed a measure to prohibit American aid to the contras. But activists in the administration were determined to continue the contra war. At first they dunned other recipients of American aid for donations; after the secret Iranian deliveries commenced, they channeled profits from those sales to the contras. The maneuver was a bald violation of both the spirit and the letter of American law — as Reagan implicitly admitted by lying about the matter when the story leaked to the press. After dissimulation became impossible, he and his aides blamed Congress: if the lawmakers had only recognized the threat the Nicaraguan regime posed to American security, they never would have cut off the contras.

But this very argument was an admission that the president had failed to make his case for a revival of the Cold War. And this failure in turn reflected the fundamental contradiction of Cold War conservatism. Reagan wanted to have things both ways: distrust of government at home, faith in government abroad. Americans had never been able to manage the feat. For most of their history they had been skeptical of government activism in domestic affairs, not to mention leery of involvement overseas. During wartime, and again during the Cold War, they had accepted the need for government activism internationally, and this acceptance had fostered a tolerance of government activism at home. But Americans had never been able to compartmentalize their trust in government — to grant it on one side of the ocean while withholding it on the other. Despite Reagan's best efforts, they refused to compartmentalize now. The Cold War was over, and Reagan — who, apparently oblivious of the bullets he was putting through his feet, kept reminding them how unworthy government was of their trust — was the last person to be able to revive it.

7

Although his efforts to resurrect the Cold War continued intermittently into his second term, by the beginning of 1984 Ronald Reagan was starting to acknowledge the likelihood of failure. In January of that year he held out the hand of cooperation to the erstwhile evil empire. "Together we can strengthen peace, reduce the level of arms, and know in doing so that we have helped fulfill the hopes and dreams of those we represent and, indeed, of people everywhere," he declared. "Let us begin now." As an actor and raconteur, Reagan had always been known for good timing, and if he came in just a little ahead of cue in this case, no one complained, for in early 1985 leadership in the Kremlin passed to Mikhail Gorbachev, whose plans for reforming the Soviet system required an end to the arms race and a re-embrace of detente. Together Gorbachev and Reagan quickly dismantled most of what remained of the superstructure of the Cold War.[1]

This pleased the liberals. Not only did they value the reduction in international tensions, but the definitive burial of the Cold War held out the prospect of a peace dividend that might be spent on various projects the defense budget had been crowding aside.

A couple of curious things, however, happened on the way to the peace bank. First, the post-Soviet world turned out to be more dangerous in its own pedestrian way than the world of the superpower era. Second, Americans were no more willing to trust Washington with new programs than they had been since the early 1970s.

To the dismay of liberals, the America of the 1990s settled into what seemed a conservative rut. Bill Clinton briefly sounded some of the old liberal themes, raising liberal hopes of a Greater Society. But when his attempt to remodel the nation's health-care system triggered a backlash that produced a Republican in-your-face victory in 1994, this New Democratic president quickly transformed himself into the Eisenhower of the Democrats, leaving liberals in the same lurch conservatives had found themselves in at the height of the Cold War.

JUST SAY YES

When Reagan first proposed talks to terminate the arms race, he had no idea what he was getting himself into. For years, arms control negotiations had proceeded glacially, when they proceeded at all. Moving from SALT I to SALT II had taken eight years, and even that tempo was too fast for the Reaganites during the heyday of neoconservative influence. But once Gorbachev found his political footing and got into the spirit of arms control, the process accelerated dramatically. The Soviet leader accepted the "zero option" for intermediate nuclear forces in Europe, reversing his predecessors' veto and thereby causing the American negotiators who had first proposed this ban on all intermediate-range missiles in Europe —

and who hadn't expected the Kremlin to accept it—to backpedal furiously.

Gorbachev pressed forward as fast as the Pentagon retreated, cornering Reagan at Reykjavik in October 1986. There he got the American president to accept a prohibition on the intermediate forces, and at once he made a far more dramatic proposal. Reagan had casually mentioned the possibility of going beyond the intermediate-range ban to the elimination of long-range missiles as well. Great idea, said Gorbachev. But why not expand it to a ban on all nuclear weapons?

Reagan's aides had dreaded this sort of situation. Even the president's staunchest defenders granted that he wasn't the master of his briefing books, especially on technical matters like nuclear weapons. It took him two years in office—two years in which he had given numerous speeches on the Soviet threat and made many important decisions on the subject, and this after a dozen years of playing Cato to the Kremlin's Carthage—to discover that the major part of Moscow's nuclear deterrent consisted of land-based intercontinental missiles. When an astonished reporter asked how he could have avoided learning such a fundamental piece of information, he responded lamely, "I never heard any one of our negotiators or any of our military people or anyone else bring up that particular point." Following a Reagan visit with Richard Nixon, who *did* know a thing or two about weapons, the former president shuddered at the ignorance of the current chief executive. "There is no way he can ever be allowed to participate in a private meeting with Gorbachev," Nixon said.[2]

So when Reagan's handlers heard of Gorbachev's proposal to ban nuclear weapons entirely, their breath caught in their throats. This was far more than any American administration had ever considered, and it would play into Moscow's traditional advantage in conventional weapons. Reagan's aides started breathing again only when they learned that the president had refused to accept Gorbachev's precondition: the canceling of SDI. For all his lack of expertise in nuclear matters, Reagan was a visionary, and at the center of his vision was a shield that would defend America against attack, the way the Atlantic and Pacific oceans had defended America against attack during the eighteenth and nineteenth centuries. Critics might call his vision unworkable, but he wasn't about to abandon it.

Yet even though the Iceland meeting failed to rid the world of most of its nuclear weapons, Reagan's last years in office yielded more progress on arms control than the terms of all seven of his postwar predecessors combined. The Intermediate Nuclear Forces treaty was signed and ratified, mandating the elimination of an entire class of weapons. Work began on a Strategic Arms Reduction Treaty, which would not simply cap numbers of the intercontinental weapons but require their substantial reduction.

The difference between the first-term Reagan and the second-term Reagan was stunning. The president who had denounced the Kremlin in biblical language became Gorbachev's best buddy, and the television footage of the two men meeting in various locations around the world reminded older viewers of Bob Hope and Bing Crosby in their "Road to . . ." days. The number of Reagan's meetings with Gorbachev almost equaled the sum of summits of all the postwar presidents before him.

Much, perhaps most, of the thaw between Washington and Moscow was due to the new direction in which Gorbachev was taking Soviet policy, but a substantial part also reflected Reagan's recognition that the new Cold War simply hadn't caught on in the United States. After all, the president's peace campaign had commenced more than a year before Gorbachev assumed power, and if the American contribution to the thaw sometimes seemed to consist chiefly of ratifying proposals that were clearly in America's interests, saying yes to something Moscow offered was more than the president had been willing to do during his first years in office.

ONE FOR THE GIPPER

By the time Reagan retired to Rancho del Cielo in the mountains above Santa Barbara, a new world was fast coming into existence. Gorbachev indicated that *glasnost* and *perestroika* applied to the East European allies as well as to the Soviet Union; evidently he hoped to learn something useful from the reforms in those countries. What he learned was that the Moscow-backed regimes there were even more unpopular than he thought, and after his spokesman explained that the Brezhnev doctrine (once socialist, always socialist) had given way to the "Sinatra doctrine" (they do it their way), the mortar rapidly began falling out of the wall that had split the continent since the late 1940s. In the case of Germany, the wall literally came tumbling down when the government of East Germany bowed to overwhelming popular pressure and allowed the free movement of its people into West Germany. The Berlin wall was transmuted in quick succession from free-fire zone to dance platform to collector's item. By the time Germany reunited in 1990 the anti-Communist revolution had swept across all of Eastern Europe, propelling the former satellites out of Moscow's orbit and, with varying speed and accuracy, onto trajectories toward democracy. The finishing fission of the Soviet empire occurred in December 1991, when, after a frustrated coup against Gorbachev, the Soviet president's democratic opponents packed him off to retirement by liquidating his country. The Soviet Union became something called the Commonwealth of Independent States, with the emphasis clearly on "independent."

Americans observed these events with astonishment and, for the most part, gratification. Conservatives claimed credit, asserting that the hard line drawn by Reagan had demonstrated the futility of continued Communist competition with the West and left Soviet leaders no choice but to capitulate. Liberals disputed this claim, countering that it was the attractions of democracy — combined, some conceded, with the allure of capitalism — that finally carried the day; if the militarization of the Cold War by the West had accomplished anything, it encouraged hard-liners in the East to respond in kind, thereby retarding reform. Those rare liberals who were willing or able to remember that the American Cold War had originally been a liberal enterprise might have trotted out such early Cold War heroes as Harry Truman and Dean Acheson if the conservatives hadn't long since claimed them for their own.

The collapse of the Soviet system prompted reflection on the fundamental issue of politics — the same issue that had divided liberals from conservatives since those terms acquired their modern meaning. Conservatives contended that the collapse of communism in Eastern Europe was part of a global recognition that in government less is more. Gorbachev in Russia simply followed the lead of Reagan in America and Margaret Thatcher in Britain; equally insightful if less well known leaders in Asia and Latin America reached the same conclusion at about the same time — that government must step out of the road and let people apply their personal energies to achieving their individual destinies in their own ways.

Liberals could hardly argue with the results of the undeniable democratizing trend, but they differed with the conservatives over what the next step should be. The United States, they held, suddenly freed from the burden of defending itself and half the globe from the threat of Soviet attack — a threat, many liberals now said, that had often been overblown — could take up the agenda of domestic public endeavors that had been pushed aside in the interest of the Reagan arms race. Some recycled Eisenhower's "Chance for Peace" speech of 1953, in which the Republican president had explained what each bomber cost in terms of schools forgone, and each aircraft carrier in hospitals; now that those bombers and carriers were no longer necessary, those schools and hospitals could finally be built. Let the conservatives gloat over winning the Cold War, many liberals concluded; we'll take the peace that follows.

There were four flaws in this vision. The first was Reagan's other legacy: the federal deficit, which towered above the landscape of American politics and cast a shadow as far into the future as even Rosy Scenario and her hopeful following of fiscal optimists could see. Any peace dividend ought to go toward reducing the deficit, conservatives asserted — and many nonconservatives agreed. Liberals grumbled; some accused the Reaganites of deliberately having driven up the deficit in order to paralyze programs for the poor for decades to come. That the occasional candid conservative conceded this point simply infuriated the liberals the more.

The second impediment to applying the peace dividend to liberal projects was that the peace it posited exploded before anyone in

Washington had a chance to start cutting checks. When the super-powers had reigned, a Pax Sovietica prevailed in Eastern Europe, and a less onerous but not conspicuously less effective Pax Americana stabilized Western Europe and most of the Western Hemisphere. Although such contentious zones as the Middle East weren't clearly within either superpower system, the evident interest and neighboring presence of those systems constrained the conflicts that arose there. The Pax Sovietica evaporated with the Soviet Union, and as it did, so did much of the motivation of the Pax Americana. Miamians still managed to get lathered over Castro in Cuba, but other areas — Yugoslavia, Central Asia, interior Africa — slipped off the radar screen of general American interest.

Yet there remained regions that could provoke as sharp a response from Washington as ever — sharper, in fact, now that American leaders no longer had to worry about a counterresponse from Moscow. When Saddam Hussein forcibly annexed Kuwait in 1990 and threatened Saudi Arabia, the specter of that obviously unfriendly fellow controlling much of the world's oil supply put the American government on high alert. George Bush dispatched a quarter-million U.S. troops to Saudi Arabia to draw a line in the sand; shortly he determined to send a quarter-million more, along with thousands of planes, missiles, ships, and other engines of war, to throw the Iraqi bully out of what he fancied Iraq's nineteenth province.

The Gulf War was brilliantly successful both in liberating Kuwait — from Saddam, if not necessarily from the Kuwaiti ruling family — and in squelching further demands for a wholesale dismantling of the American military. Soviet Union or no Soviet Union, challenges to American interests persisted, and the United States needed to be able to respond. To be sure, marginal reductions were possible, and in a budget of hundreds of billions of dollars, the margins weren't peanuts. But the dividends from defense downsizing wouldn't even approach the numbers the liberals had already spent in their dreams.

IT'S THE STUPID ECONOMY

The third impediment to a liberal peace dividend was the recession that hit the American economy during the second half of the Bush administration. The dip wasn't unexpected; even those who trumpeted the final triumph of the free market conceded that the business cycle hadn't been defeated. The surprise wasn't that the recession arrived, the capitalist triumphalists said, but that it had tarried so long—a matter that seemed to afford additional evidence of the power of the invisible hand.

In politics, timing is everything; voters balance their books, if not every day, at least at every election. Had the recession occurred a year earlier, Bush probably would have waltzed to victory in 1992. But the recession took the luster off his Gulf victory, and from an astronomical 89 percent (the highest in Gallup history) at the time of the defeat of Saddam, the president's approval rating plummeted to a Carteresque 29 percent in the summer of 1992. As it turned out, the recession had ended by the November elections, but the data delineating the recovery were too late and incomplete to make much of a case for incumbency.[3]

Compounding Bush's problem was the cleverness of Bill Clinton's campaign. Clinton early made a strategic decision to concede foreign policy to the president and to harass him on domestic affairs, especially the economy. In the event, Clinton managed the unlikely feat of turning Bush's foreign-policy triumphs — the Gulf War and the defeat of European communism — against him by arguing that the president should have been minding matters at home rather than saving the world. Under other circumstances — for example, under the circumstances of the Cold War — Clinton's charges would have fallen flat. But with little to worry about overseas, Americans found it easy to obsess about their domestic ills.

By the standards of other industrial countries, the American economy was in sturdy shape. American unemployment was consistently among the lowest in the industrialized world; even in the recession year of 1992, the American jobless rate of 7.5 percent was substantially lower than those of Britain, France, and Canada (it possibly was lower than that of Germany as well, although it was hard to tell because the Germans were still trying to figure out how to calculate the statistics for the former East Germany). And the American standard of living remained the envy of the world. A few countries had higher numerical average incomes, but in terms of what those incomes could actually purchase, the United States remained the class of the globe.[4]

Yet Americans, believing themselves exceptional, have rarely measured themselves by the yardstick of other nations; instead they have measured themselves against themselves. And by historical American standards the economy did indeed give cause for concern during the early 1990s. Most indicators revealed that the historic growth curve of the American economy had flattened out during the 1970s and never regained its healthy slope. The economy continued to produce jobs, but these were not the blue-collar manufacturing careers that had anchored the industrializing nation; the bulk of the new slots were in the service sector, which was notorious for low pay, meager benefits, and high turnover. Family income held about steady, but only because more people — chiefly married women — were working. The economy had pockets of exuberance, especially in the high-tech areas, but the obverse of the exuberance was the uncertainty that afflicted millions of workers who didn't know from one month to the next if they would be outsourced, part-timed, RIFfed, or simply expended. And to make matters worse, by most evidence the gap between those at the top of the economy and those at the bottom was growing. The boardrooms garnered bonuses and stock options while the mailrooms scrabbled from paycheck to paycheck. The promise of American life had always been that each generation would be better off than its predecessor. As long as it was kept, this promise diminished the resentment of the lower classes for the higher. Who cared how the Rockefellers lived as long as everyone was getting richer?

By the early 1990s the promise seemed to have been broken. The generation that followed the postwar baby boom was the first to have reason to expect that its living standard wouldn't match that of its parents. The boomers often criticized their children — or perhaps the children of other boomers — for narrowly utilitarian attitudes toward education; where was the activist spirit that had infused the campuses during the 1960s? Although the Generation Xers often lacked the perspective to answer completely, one explanation was that when good jobs were tight and good grades imperative, there simply wasn't time for protests and strikes and the other extracurriculars their parents had indulged in.

In certain respects, however, the youngsters had it better than their elders. The children didn't know what they were missing, while the parents did. And all the corporate reshuffling and reorganization was especially hard on mid-career managerial types who had grown accustomed to a style of life they would have a difficult time reproducing if they were laid off. Many *were* laid off, and for each one who was, a dozen lay awake nights wondering when the bell would toll for them.

THE REVOLUTION OF FALLING EXPECTATIONS

These were the people to whom candidate Clinton spoke when he said he "felt their pain." Whether or not he really did, he gave a convincing impression. He was a master performer, and being a generation younger than Bush or Reagan, he came across as far more in touch with the concerns of his contemporaries.

Whether he would have won without the help of Ross Perot was a matter pollsters, pundits, and political scientists debated afterward. But whatever it did to boost Clinton and doom Bush, the candidacy of the Texas billionaire testified to the continuing popular suspicion of government. Perot may have been an honest populist, a crazy capitalist, or simply someone whose money allowed him to buy his fifteen minutes of fame — and his 19 percent of the vote — but he certainly was not a professional pol. And each vote for Perot, whether stolen from Bush or from Clinton, was decidedly a vote against government.

Not since Woodrow Wilson had a presidential winner fallen so far short of a popular majority as Clinton — but Clinton quickly demonstrated he was no Wilson. His ideas on resolving America's difficulties had been vague before November 1992, and they grew hardly more distinct after January 1993. The major domestic initiative of his first term — an attempt to reorganize the health-care system, and in the process substantially increase the federal role therein — went flaming down to defeat. The usual suspects — diverse lobbyists for the status quo — naturally assaulted the president's proposal, but what really killed it was the fundamental lack of support on the part of voters. As uneasy as many people were regarding the changes in doctor-patient relations during the previous decade, most had little confidence that the interposition of the federal government would improve matters.

This was the fourth impediment to the liberal peace dividend, and the most telling of all. Twenty years after Vietnam shattered the Cold War consensus, spawning Watergate and destroying popular faith in government, Americans had conspicuously little confidence that Washington could accomplish much good in their lives. In March 1993 a poll conducted by Gallup, CNN television, and *USA Today* queried a cross section of Americans as to whether the federal government should use its power more vigorously to promote the well-being of the American people; by a resounding margin of more than two to one (65 percent to 31 percent) respondents rejected the proposition. Nearly four out of ten respondents (38 percent) said Washington had too much power as it was.[5]

And the popular mood grew only more sour. As the congressional campaign of 1994 concentrated voters' attention on the performance of their legislators, it also concentrated their annoyance. A poll taken a few weeks before the election revealed that public dissatisfaction with Congress had reached 70 percent. Another poll asked respondents to name an elected official they admired; 60 percent couldn't identify a single one.[6]

The popular antipathy toward government produced a seismic shift on Capitol Hill. Republicans regained control of the Senate, which although surprising wasn't inconceivable, in that it had happened the decade before. More shocking was the GOP's seizure of the House, the likes of which had last occurred during Eisenhower's first term. The key to the Republican success was the "contract with America" — a grab bag of ten promises promoted by Newt Gingrich of Georgia, who became the House speaker in the new Congress. Predictably, the package was a thoroughgoing indictment of government. It called for a balanced-budget constitutional amendment and a line-item veto, both of which could be expected to restrain federal spending. It pledged to push for a constitutional amendment to limit congressional terms. It endorsed welfare reform, a middle-class tax cut, a cut in the capital gains tax, reductions in federal paperwork and in unfunded mandates (orders from Washington to carry out federal policies for free), cost-benefit analysis of federal regulations, reimbursement to landowners for reductions in property values caused by federal decrees, and restrictions on the right of investors to sue companies. It wasn't at all clear that voters who punched the Republican ticket endorsed every one of the contract's clauses, but it was undeniable that they supported the general tenor of the message.

Clinton certainly got the message. In his state of the union address in January 1995 he acknowledged that "our Government, once a champion of national purpose, is now seen by many as simply a captive of narrow interests, putting more burdens on our citizens rather than equipping them to get ahead." He proposed junking the old way of conducting the public business, in favor of a "new covenant." "The old way dispensed services through large, top-down, inflexible bureaucracies. The New Covenant way would shift these resources and decisionmaking from bureaucrats to citizens, injecting choice and competition and individual responsibility into national policy. . . . We must not ask Government to do what we should do for ourselves." Clinton boasted of the number of federal programs and government jobs he had eliminated already, and he promised to eliminate more. "We have to cut yesterday's Government to help solve tomorrow's problems." Then he wisely walked out of the Capitol and let the Republicans have their day.[7]

Actually they had their hundred days. In a symbolic riposte to the signature start of the New Deal, Speaker Gingrich set a hundred-day goal for fulfilling the House's end of the Republican contract. The large class of Republican freshman rallied to their leader, and they made more progress toward achieving that conservative goal than anyone could have imagined just six months before. The lower chamber approved the balanced-budget amendment, the line-item veto, welfare reform, tax cuts, and restrictions on unfunded mandates, federal paperwork, and investor lawsuits.

As expected by almost everyone with Washington experience — including Clinton but not including many of those Republican freshman — the Senate was in rather less of a rush to shake up the status quo. The upper house readily seconded the line-item veto and the curb on unfunded mandates and federal paperwork, but in keeping with its self-conferred reputation as the most deliberative body in the world, it considered the other items more carefully. Several simply stalled in committee or succumbed to the long-windedness Senate rules allow; one of the handful of measures that came to an up-or-down decision — the balanced-budget amendment — fell short by a single vote (which became two votes when Senate majority leader Robert Dole tactically altered his aye to nay).

The excitement over the Republican contract dissipated further as Congress took up the substantive business of governing — the budget. The fire-eaters in the House approved deep cuts in social, educational, and environmental programs. The Senate again took a more moderate line, and by now Clinton had regained his voice, which he used to threaten vetoes of the more extreme measures being bandied by the House. The public grew disgusted and pinned most of the blame on Congress. Polls taken at the beginning of the 1995 congressional session had indicated a sense of favorable anticipation; they now registered sharp dissatisfaction. One survey conducted in November revealed an approval rating of Congress on the budget of just 21 percent, against 71 percent disapproval.[8]

Things got even worse when the budget impasse led to a shutdown of the federal government. First-term Republicans in the House determined to force Clinton to accept a steep glide to a balanced budget, accomplished largely through cuts in social programs. Clinton vowed to veto any such package, and time ran out on the government's spending authority. A November shutdown sent 800,000 federal workers home; following a temporary cease-fire and recall, some 260,000 "non-essential" workers were again furloughed the following month. Apparently some of the Republican radicals thought the shutdown would demonstrate that nearly all federal workers were non-essential, but when holiday tourists encountered locked gates at national parks and business executives were compelled to cancel trips overseas for lack of up-to-date passports — and when voters told pollsters that the Republicans were chiefly to blame for this sorry state of affairs — a compromise started to seem attractive.

The odd thing was that it was Clinton who did the most conspicuous compromising. "The era of big government is over," he declared, and underscored his remarks by accepting the Republicans' seven-year timetable for balancing the budget. In the interest of the approaching elections, the two sides tacitly agreed not to inquire too closely into the figures that informed each other's assessments of what constituted balance. Until after November 1996, smoke, mirrors, and promises would be acceptable fiscal tools.[9]

WAITING FOR LEFTY

Perhaps surprisingly, and in stark contrast to the previous couple of election years, 1996 was kind to incumbents. Charity's chief cause was the relatively robust condition of the American economy — relative both to the American economy of the early 1990s and to the economies of other countries. Corporate restructurings weren't so drastic or frequent as of late, and the double-digit unemployment that plagued most of America's industrialized partners made the American jobless figure of 6 percent (and falling) seem positively praiseworthy.

The most virulent of the anti-government zeal that had ousted incumbents in 1992 and 1994 had spent its force. Newt Gingrich insufficiently appreciated how the Republican congressional victory changed things: his tirades against government rang hollow now that the Republicans *were* the government. (Ronald Reagan had been reelected in 1984 by running against government, but Gingrich was no Reagan.) Moreover, Clinton again demonstrated his virtuosity — not to be confused with his virtue, as indeed it rarely was — in appealing to voters. Having made himself into a Democratic version of Dwight Eisenhower, he gave voters little reason to replace him with that other son of the Kansas prairie, Robert Dole. They didn't, returning Clinton to office, along with Republican majorities in the Senate and House.

A few people who hadn't been paying attention thought reelection would free Clinton to be his genuine liberal self, but if anything it reinforced his conservative tendencies. He apparently reconciled himself to the fact that his principal legacy might be balancing the federal budget, an aspiration (let alone an achievement) not conspicuously associated with Democrats since Franklin Roosevelt had hectored Herbert Hoover for fiscal irresponsibility — and upon election revealed he had just been kidding.

The balanced budget (and eventually much more) indeed arrived during Clinton's second term — yet by the time it did, most observers, and probably the president himself, realized he would be remembered not for black ink but for a blue dress. The tawdry spectacle of Clinton's impeachment trial diminished nearly everyone's opinion of government still further; the only question was whether the actions of Kenneth Starr and the Republicans in pursuit of the president were more disgraceful and incompetent than the actions for which the president was pursued.

The Starr investigation momentarily blurred the distinction (as it had often been blurred in the past) between the genuine conservatism of small government and the pseudo-conservatism of "family values." Those liberals who hadn't apostatized took heart from the ultimate failure of the Republican sex police — but that was all they could take heart from in two terms that underlined how thoroughly entrenched conservatism (the real version) was in American politics. For nearly twenty years Democrats had complained that the Reagan deficits precluded addressing important national problems; by the time the deficits vanished, so had the Democrats' desire to address those problems. In response to Republican demands for tax cuts and a further diminution of government, the Democratic president could only unimaginatively call for using the surplus to strengthen the Social Security trust fund.

Yet not even that centerpiece of the welfare state was immune to conservative tinkering. After several years of the bullest bull market in Wall Street memory, many Democrats — including Clinton — joined Republicans in deriding the modest returns the trust fund was realizing from government securities, and advocating placing at least part of the funds in the private market. Social Security had long been considered the third rail of American politics, but with the plug pulled on liberalism, its capacity to shock had been drastically diminished.

In other areas the conservative trend was equally evident. The federal government had essentially abandoned the field of antitrust; the show trial of the late 1990s, of Microsoft Corporation for predatory practices, was rendered largely irrelevant by the renewed frenzy of mergers undertaken — and countenanced by the Justice Department — in the name of global competitiveness. The 1996 Federal Agricultural Improvement and Reform Act sent off toward the sunset one of the oldest and most deeply rooted federal responsibilities: for management of the agricultural industry. (This was one of the responsibilities Eisenhower had pronounced untouchable in the mid-1950s.) The Personal Responsibility and Work Opportunity Reconciliation Act of the same year fulfilled a Clinton promise to "end welfare as we know it," by terminating federal responsibility for welfare and handing this basic problem of poverty over to the states.

The election of 2000 underlined the essential conservatism of the American system. George W. Bush unsurprisingly called for massive tax cuts and for private-sector solutions to the problems of Social Security (set up private accounts) and Medicare (let private insurance provide prescription drug coverage). Al Gore occasionally reminded voters that the general prosperity of the 1990s had exacerbated the division between rich and poor, but he took pains to distinguish himself from anything like the liberalism his party had espoused under Lyndon Johnson. "I don't ever want to see another era of big government," the vice president declared two weeks before the election. Evidently attempting to outflank Bush on the right, Gore continued, "In this tale of two candidates, I'm the one who believes in limited government, and I have believed in it long before it was fashionable to do so in the Democratic Party. I don't believe there's a government solution to every problem. I don't believe any government program can replace the responsibility of parents, the hard work of families or the innovation of industry."[10]

With both candidates fleeing liberalism like the political plague it remained, the voters delivered a split decision. Gore got the satisfaction of knowing that a plurality of voters preferred his limited vision of government responsibility for the country's welfare; Bush (with an even more limited vision, notwithstanding Gore's protests) had to settle for the White House.

All this was very puzzling to many of those who had come of age with Clinton and Gore and Bush, and come of age thinking liberalism was the default setting of American politics. Their mistake was natural enough, for they were the generation of the Cold War, and of Cold War liberalism. For a quarter-century Americans had grown used to looking to Washington for leadership, first in matters of national security and then, as the Cold War suffused nearly all areas of American life, in such previously domestic matters as education, transportation, civil rights, and health care. As long as the Cold War proceeded successfully for the United States, popular confidence in government appeared justified. A people accustomed to depending on government to protect them from nuclear annihilation didn't find it much of a stretch to look to government to address such comparatively minor challenges as an anachronistic system of race relations and lingering economic inequality.

Yet when the war in Vietnam turned sour, revealing the lack of both good judgment and basic integrity on the part of American officials, the skein of popular trust in government unraveled. Vietnam begot Watergate, which begot investigations that revealed that the deception hadn't started with Nixon but ran back to the origins of the Cold War. Not surprisingly, Americans responded as people often do when they discover that they have been played for fools: they withdrew their trust and vowed not to be fooled again. To many of the generation that had known only the Cold War, the conservative reaction that produced the presidency of Ronald Reagan seemed anomalous: a temporary swing of the pendulum from left to right. Soon enough, they reasoned, the pendulum would swing back and liberalism would regain its former ascendancy.

But in fact it was the liberalism of the Cold War era that was the anomaly. The appropriate image wasn't a pendulum but a balloon, one held aloft by the confidence in government the successful prosecution of the Cold War inspired. When Vietnam destroyed that confidence, the balloon deflated, and expectations of government descended to their traditional low level. Pendulums swing back on their own; balloons require refilling.

This was why liberalism was not likely to revive any time soon. In modern America, liberalism was a consequence of the Cold War, a side effect of the national security state. The Cold War was now dead and buried, and Americans had reverted to their historic skepticism of big government. If the past was any guide, another serious threat to American security would be required to displace this skepticism. As of the beginning of 2001, such a threat seemed years or decades in the future. Perhaps Russia would regain its grip in the twenty-first century and once more endanger Europe — and through Europe, America. Perhaps China would transform its growing economic power into a force more martial, thereby jeopardizing the stability of East Asia and the Pacific. Global warming might someday swamp America's seacoasts.

But these were remote threats, which might never move much

closer than the distance of bother. And until they did, or until some other challenge surfaced that caused Americans to put their reliance in Washington as they had during earlier periods of national peril, it was difficult to see how — or why — Americans would alter the attitudes toward government they had developed over two centuries.

AFTERWORD: THE LAZARUS OPTION

The purpose of history is not to make people happy; it is to make them wiser. Yet some find history — or at least parts of it — a happier hunting ground than others do. To the extent anyone infers encouragement from the foregoing chapters, such heartened souls are bound to be conservatives. History would seem to be on their side, and therefore they on its. (That this was where Marxists always claimed to be — until history ran them down — is perhaps food for conservative thought.)

Liberals may not be as discouraged as they ought to be, doubtless partly because some won't buy the argument proffered here. They will place more faith in Franklin Roosevelt as a liberal, for example, and see the New Deal — rather than the Cold War — as the wellspring of postwar liberalism. Extrapolating backward, they will include Woodrow Wilson and Theodore Roosevelt in the liberal embrace and interpret modern liberalism as a response to permanent changes in the domestic American economy that began in the nineteenth century, rather than as a reaction to a temporary (if protracted) reconfiguration of the international system after World War II.

Certain classes of explanations of the world are essentially all-or-nothing affairs. Creationism, for instance, posits a divine intelligence behind the origin of pretty much everything that exists; it would be an odd creationist who claimed that God made mammals, bacteria, and asteroids while leaving amphibians, protozoa, and quasars to evolve on their own.

Other explanatory models are more syncretic, allowing theory-shoppers to buy a little or a lot rather than all or none. Most historical explanations are of this nature. Was the Civil War about slavery or states' rights? The answer is: both. (The Civil War is *still* about both — as continuing squabbles over the Confederate battle flag demonstrate.)

The model of American liberalism supplied in the previous chapters is similarly syncretic. At full strength it asserts (as those chapters asserted) that the Cold War was essential to the flowering of American liberalism, and that when the Cold War paradigm broke down, so necessarily did liberalism. Liberals (and others) may reject this version yet still accept a milder form: that the Cold War, if not strictly essential to liberalism, at least facilitated the liberals' post-war ascendancy. (Of course, liberals may reject this milder version, too, but that would be embracing contrariness for the sake of contrariness.)

Swallowing their medicine diluted, liberals might consider how to reconstruct a liberal majority. They could start with a recognition that the reason the American people turned to government during the Cold War was that national security is an issue unarguably in the federal domain. Put simply, no one does defense like the feds (the Second Amendment and assorted militia groups notwithstanding). Americans accepted this fact — as they had since the Revolutionary War — and as long as Washington did a good job on defense during the Cold War, they were willing to trust Washington on issues arguably related to national security.

In the absence of a renewed security threat, liberals will need to identify another issue Washington clearly does better than anyone else. (Of course, in the *presence* of a renewed security threat, the liberals will once again be called to power—Q.E.D.) This other issue might be health care or the environment or income inequality or something entirely different. (That just about any issue besides national security starts an argument indicates the crux of the liberals' dilemma.) But whatever the issue identified, to the extent government addresses it successfully, Americans' traditional skepticism of government will diminish.

The good news for liberals is that although Americans are conservatives, their conservatism is pragmatic rather than ideological. What government does well they are willing to let government do. In the past this has been, preeminently, national security and, secondarily, what could be hung on the security theme. In the future it may be something else. Finding that something is up to the liberal imagination—and the liberal performance.

Notes are employed for direct quotations and specific statistics only. Sources employed more generally may be found in the essay on sources.

CHAPTER 1: A NATION OF SKEPTICS

1. Gordon S. Wood, *The Creation of the American Republic* (New York, 1972 ed.), 272.
2. *The Federalist Papers,* ed. Andrew Hacker (New York, 1964 ed.), 154 (Number 84).
3. Jonathan Elliot, ed., *The Debates in the Several State Conventions on the Adoption of the Federal Constitution* (Philadelphia, 1901), 4:315 (Lincoln); Max Farrand, ed., *Records of the Federal Convention of 1787* (New Haven, 1923), 3:291 (Martin).
4. Jack N. Rakove, *James Madison and the Creation of the American Republic* (Glenview, Ill., 1990), 81–82.
5. Lance Banning, *The Jeffersonian Persuasion* (Ithaca, N.Y., 1978), 275.
6. Robert Remini, *Andrew Jackson and the Course of American Freedom* (New York, 1981), 366.

7. Tocqueville, *Democracy in America,* ed. Richard D. Heffner (New York, 1980 ed.), 1:82–83, 87, 271.

8. Richard Hofstadter and Beatrice K. Hofstadter, eds., *Great Issues in American History* (New York, 1982 ed.), 3:142.

9. Joseph Bucklin Bishop, *Theodore Roosevelt and His Time* (New York, 1926 ed.), 1:212.

10. Herbert Croly, *The Promise of American Life* (Cambridge, Mass., 1965 ed.), 214; *The Works of Theodore Roosevelt* (New York, 1925), 19:382–88. The book Roosevelt was citing was Charles R. Van Hise, *Concentration and Control: A Solution of the Trust Problem in the United States* (New York, 1912).

11. Wilson, *The New Freedom* (New York, 1913), 169–70, 200–202.

12. William E. Leuchtenburg, *Franklin Roosevelt and the New Deal* (New York, 1963), 10–11.

13. Ibid., 235.

14. Arthur M. Schlesinger, Jr., *The Coming of the New Deal* (Boston, 1958), 308–9.

15. George H. Gallup, *The Gallup Poll: Public Opinion, 1935–1971* (New York, 1972), Oct. 20 and Dec. 15, 1935; Feb. 2 and Nov. 29, 1936; June 29, 1938; Jan. 6, 1939.

CHAPTER 2: BENEATH THE EAGLE'S WINGS

1. James M. McPherson, *Battle Cry of Freedom: The Civil War Era* (New York, 1988), 445–46.

2. Shelby Foote, *The Civil War* (New York, 1963), 2:152.

3. McPherson, *Battle Cry,* 289.

4. Charles A. Beard and Mary R. Beard, *The Rise of American Civilization* (New York, 1934 ed.), 2:81.

5. Frederick Palmer, *Newton D. Baker: America at War* (New York, 1931), 1:120; Edward M. Coffman, *The War to End All Wars: The American Military Experience in World War I* (New York, 1968), 8.

6. David M. Kennedy, *Over Here: The First World War and American Society* (New York, 1980), 145 (Creel); H. C. Peterson and Gilbert C. Fite, *Opponents of War* (Madison, Wis., 1957), 23 (Wilson).

7. *New York Times,* Mar. 13, 1917 (Pinchot); Peterson and Fite, *Opponents of War,* 22 (Clark).

8. Robert D. Cuff, *The War Industries Board* (Baltimore, 1973), 102 (House); Daniel R. Beaver, *Newton D. Baker and the American War Effort* (Lincoln, Neb., 1966), 108.

9. Cuff, *War Industries Board,* 105.

10. George Creel, *How We Advertised America* (New York, 1920), 86–87; James R. Mock and Cedric Larson, *Words That Won the War* (Princeton, 1939), 124.

11. Kennedy, *Over Here,* 108.

12. *Historical Statistics of the United States* (Washington, D.C., 1975), 1104–11.

13. Peterson and Fite, *Opponents of War,* 14 (Gregory) and 95 (Burleson).

14. Ronald Schaffer, *America in the Great War: The Rise of the War Welfare State* (New York, 1991), 17.

15. Richard R. Lingeman, *Don't You Know There's a War On?* (New York, 1976 ed.), 227.

16. Richard Polenberg, ed., *America at War* (Englewood Cliffs, N.J., 1968), 17.

17. Ibid., 92.

18. Donald M. Nelson, *Arsenal of Democracy* (New York, 1946), 342 (Nelson); Polenberg, *America at War,* 24 (Witte).

19. Lingeman, *Don't You Know,* 121–22.

20. Geoffrey Perrett, *Days of Sadness, Years of Triumph* (New York, 1973), 117.

21. *Historical Statistics,* 224, 1105.

CHAPTER 3: THE WAR THAT NEVER ENDED

1. George F. Kennan, *Memoirs, 1925–50* (New York, 1967), 557.

2. Harry S. Truman, *Memoirs,* vol. 2: *Years of Trial and Hope* (New York, 1965 ed.), 124, 128.

3. *Public Papers of the Presidents* (hereafter *Public Papers*), Mar. 12, 1947.

4. James T. Patterson, *Mr. Republican: A Biography of Robert A. Taft* (Boston, 1972), 151–52, 157, 248, 385, 437.

5. *Congressional Record,* July 11, 1949.

6. *The Private Papers of Senator Vandenberg,* ed. Arthur H. Vandenberg, Jr. (Boston, 1952), 498, 501.

7. *American Cold War Strategy: Interpreting* NSC 68, ed. Ernest R. May (Boston, 1993) (includes the text of NSC-68).

8. Dean Acheson, *Present at the Creation: My Years in the State Department* (New York, 1969), 374.

9. Alonzo L. Hamby, *Liberalism and Its Challengers* (New York, 1992 ed.), 113.

10. Patterson, *Mr. Republican,* 480.

CHAPTER 4: LIBERALS ALL!

1. *Department of State Bulletin,* Jan. 25, 1954.
2. H. W. Brands, *Cold Warriors: Eisenhower's Generation and American Foreign Policy* (New York, 1988), 67.
3. H. W. Brands, "The Age of Vulnerability: Eisenhower and the National Insecurity State," *American Historical Review* 94 (October 1989), 970.
4. Alonzo L. Hamby, *Liberalism and Its Challengers* (New York, 1992 ed.), 121.
5. NSC 68 in *American Cold War Strategy: Interpreting* NSC 68, ed. Ernest R. May (Boston, 1993).
6. Stephen E. Ambrose, *Eisenhower: The President* (New York, 1984), 115.
7. Mary L. Dudziac, *Cold War Civil Rights: Race and the Image of American Democracy* (Princeton, N.J. 2000), 100; Brands, *Cold Warriors,* 171.
8. Brands, *Cold Warriors,* 171.
9. *Public Papers,* Sept. 24, 1957.
10. *Public Papers,* Jan. 20, 1961.
11. George H. Gallup, The *Gallup Poll: Public Opinion, 1935–1971* (New York, 1972), Oct. 10 and Dec. 5, 1962.
12. James N. Giglio, *The Presidency of John F. Kennedy* (Lawrence, Kan., 1991), 131; *Public Papers,* Apr. 11, 1962.
13. Thomas C. Reeves, *A Question of Character* (New York, 1991), 332; Allen J. Matusow, *The Unraveling of America* (New York, 1984), 41.
14. *Public Papers,* Dec. 14, 1962.
15. *Public Papers,* June 11, 1962.
16. *Public Papers,* Dec. 14, 1962.

17. *Public Papers,* May 25, 1961.

18. Robert Dallek, *Flawed Giant: Lyndon Johnson and His Times, 1961–1973* (New York, 1998), 196.

19. *Public Papers,* Jan. 4, 1965.

20. *Public Papers,* Mar. 15, 1965.

21. Doris Kearns (Goodwin), *Lyndon Johnson and the American Dream* (New York, 1991 ed.), 252–53.

22. Ibid., 251–52.

CHAPTER 5: FROM HUBRIS TO SUTTEE

1. Larry Berman, *Lyndon Johnson's War* (New York, 1989), 110.

2. Stanley Karnow, *Vietnam* (New York, 1984 ed.), 41.

3. Richard Nixon, *The Memoirs of Richard Nixon* (New York, 1978), 449–51.

4. H. W. Brands, *The Specter of Neutralism: The United States and the Emergence of the Third World, 1947–1960* (New York, 1989), 5.

5. *Weekly Compilation of Presidential Documents,* June 5, 1972.

6. Nixon, *Memoirs,* 353.

7. *Public Papers,* Aug. 13, 1969; Joan Hoff, *Nixon Reconsidered* (New York, 1994), 67 (Garment).

8. William Safire, *Before the Fall* (New York, 1975), 592; Tom Wicker, *One of Us: Richard Nixon and the American Dream* (New York, 1995), 515.

9. *Public Papers,* Dec. 8, 1969.

10. Bruce Oudes, ed., *From: The President: Richard Nixon's Secret Files* (New York, 1990 ed.), 271–72.

11. Ibid., 270–71.

12. Nixon, *Memoirs,* 513–15.

13. Ibid., 889.

14. George W. Ball, *The Past Has Another Pattern* (New York, 1982), 285–86.

CHAPTER 6: THE CONTRADICTIONS
OF COLD WAR CONSERVATISM

1. Interview first published in November 1976, reprinted in *The Playboy Interview,* ed. G. Barry Golson (New York, 1981), 488.

2. Jimmy Carter, *Keeping Faith* (Toronto, 1982), 74.

3. Burton I. Kaufman, *The Presidency of James Earl Carter, Jr.* (Lawrence, Kan., 1993), 33.

4. Carter, *Keeping Faith,* 27.

5. *Public Papers,* May 22, 1977.

6. *American Foreign Policy Basic Documents, 1977–1980,* 811.

7. *The Gallup Poll: Public Opinion 1980* (Wilmington, Del., 1981) (hereafter *Gallup Poll* with appropriate year), Aug. 1, 1980.

8. Lou Cannon, *President Reagan: The Role of a Lifetime* (New York, 1992 ed.), 26.

9. *Public Papers,* Jan. 20, 1981.

10. *Public Papers,* Jan. 29, 1981; Mar. 8, 1983.

11. Cannon, *President Reagan,* 288–89.

12. *Public Papers,* Jan. 29, 1981.

13. *Gallup Poll,* Feb. 9, 1984.

14. H. W. Brands, *The Devil We Knew: Americans and the Cold War* (New York, 1993), 174.

15. Ibid.

16. David A. Stockman, *The Triumph of Politics: The Inside Story of the Reagan Revolution* (New York, 1987 ed.), 409.

17. *Public Papers,* June 30, 1985.

CHAPTER 7: NUNC DIMITTIS

1. *Public Papers,* Jan. 16, 1984.

2. Lou Cannon, *President Reagan: The Role of a Lifetime* (New York, 1992 ed.), 29; Jonathan Aiken, *Nixon* (New York, 1993), 562.

3. *Gallup Poll 1991,* Mar. 6, 1991 and Aug. 4, 1992.

4. *Statistical Abstract of the United States 1996,* 842.

5. *Gallup Poll 1993,* appendix: p. 237.

6. *New York Times,* Oct. 16 and Nov. 3, 1994.

7. *Public Papers,* Jan. 24, 1995.

8. *Congressional Quarterly Almanac 1995,* 1–11.

9. *Public Papers,* Jan. 23, 1996.

10. *New York Times,* Oct. 25, 2000.

A WORD ON SOURCES

Because this book covers such a large sweep of American history, any attempt to indicate relevant sources must be highly selective. What follows is indeed selective but — the author hopes — not overly idiosyncratic. And it identifies the works he found especially useful.

Regarding liberalism: The good-riddance school of accounting for liberalism's demise includes Charles Murray, *Losing Ground: American Social Policy, 1950–1980* (New York, 1984); Robert H. Bork, *Slouching Towards Gomorrah: Modern Liberalism and American Decline* (New York, 1996); John Kekes, *Against Liberalism* (Ithaca, N.Y., 1997); and Lee Edwards, *The Conservative Revolution: The Movement That Remade America* (New York, 1999). The lamentations for liberalism's decline are less numerous and less explicit, largely because most liberals can't bring themselves to admit their cause is lost. But two worth noting are Gareth Davies, *From Opportunity to Entitlement: The Transformation of Great Society Liberalism* (Lawrence, Kan., 1996); and Russell Jacoby, *The End of Utopia: Politics and Culture in an Age of Apathy* (New York, 1999).

On the more general subject of liberalism in modern American history, the reader might start with Alonzo L. Hamby, *Liberalism and Its Challengers: From F.D.R. to Bush* (New York, 1992) — a book that interprets liberalism quite differently than the present volume does. Michael S. Sherry, *In the Shadow of War: The United States since the 1930s* (New Haven, 1995), describes the past six decades of American history in terms of a militarization of American life — an approach complementary to the one given here, but distinct in important ways. James Patterson, *Grand Expectations: The United States, 1945–1974* (New York, 1996), is more comprehensive than interpretive. Arthur M. Schlesinger Jr., *The Cycles of American History* (Boston, 1986), sees a natural and recurring rhythm to reform and reaction. Garry Wills, *A Necessary Evil: A History of American Distrust of Government* (New York, 1999), supports some of the present book's account of Americans' long-standing skepticism of government. George Packer, *Blood of the Liberals* (New York, 2000), injects a personal — to wit, familial — element into the rise and fall of liberalism. Stephen M. Gillon, *That's Not What We Meant to Do: Reform and Its Unintended Consequences in the Twentieth Century* (New York, 2000), charts the gap between promise and performance.

On broader issues: The best survey of the Revolutionary period is Robert Middlekauff, *The Glorious Cause: The American Revolution, 1763–1789 (New York, 1982)*. James M. McPherson, *Battle Cry of Freedom: The Civil War Era* (New York, 1988), is similarly authoritative on its subject. Populism is well covered in Lawrence Goodwyn, *Democratic Promise: The Populist Moment in America* (New York, 1976). Standard works on progressivism (and Populism) include Richard Hofstadter, *The Age of Reform: From Bryan to F.D.R.* (New York, 1955), and Robert H. Wiebe, *The Search for Order, 1877–1920* (New York, 1967). On America during World War I, the best book is David M. Kennedy, *Over Here: The First World War and American Society* (New York, 1980). Kennedy is also the author of the most definitive and up-to-date treatment of the Great Depression and World War II: *Freedom from Fear: The American People in Depression and War, 1929–1945* (New York, 1999). On World War II at home, see also John Morton Blum, *V Was For Victory: Politics and American Culture During World War II* (New York, 1976).

On the early years of the Cold War and the emergence of the Cold War consensus, see Alonzo L. Hamby, *Beyond the New Deal: Harry S. Truman and American Liberalism* (New York, 1973); John Patrick Diggins, *The Proud Decades: America in War and Peace, 1941– 1960* (New York, 1988); William L. O'Neill, *American High: The Years of Confidence, 1945–1960* (New York, 1986); and James Patterson, *Grand Expectations*. H. W. Brands, *The Devil We Knew: Americans and the Cold War* (New York, 1993), covers the entire Cold War, through the early 1990s.

Stephen E. Ambrose, *Eisenhower: The President* (New York, 1984), is the best-informed biographical study of the Republican president. David Halberstam, *The Fifties* (New York, 1993), is both informative and entertaining.

The Kennedy and Johnson years are covered in Allen J. Matusow, *The Unraveling of America: A History of Liberalism in the 1960s* (New York, 1984); James N. Giglio, *The Presidency of John F. Kennedy* (Lawrence, Kan., 1991); Robert Dallek, *Flawed Giant: Lyndon Johnson and His Times, 1961–1973* (New York, 1998); and Irving Bernstein, *Guns or Butter: The Presidency of Lyndon Johnson* (New York, 1996). Dozens of good books deal with the Vietnam War; for years (and three editions) the place to begin has been George C. Herring, *America's Longest War: The United States and Vietnam, 1950–1975* (New York, 1996).

The disintegration of the Cold War consensus under Nixon plays a large part in Stephen E. Ambrose, *Nixon*, 3 vols. (New York, 1987–1991). Joan Hoff, *Nixon Reconsidered* (New York, 1994), shows Nixon's liberal side. Stanley I. Kutler, *The Wars of Watergate: The Last Crisis of Richard Nixon* (New York, 1992), gives no quarter to its subject. David Frum, *How We Got Here: The 70's, the Decade that Brought You Modern Life (for Better or Worse)* (New York, 2000), is differently opinionated. A breathtakingly comprehensive account of detente (and what followed) is Raymond L. Garthoff, *Détente and Confrontation: American-Soviet Relations from Nixon to Reagan* (Washington, 1994).

Jimmy Carter is covered in Burton I. Kaufman, *The Presidency of James Earl Carter, Jr.* (Lawrence, Kan., 1993). John Ehrman measures the neoconservatives in *The Rise of Neoconservatism: Intellectuals and Foreign Affairs, 1945–1994* (New Haven, Conn., 1995). The most insightful treatment of the Reagan phenomenon is Lou Cannon, *President Reagan: The Role of a Lifetime* (New York, 1991 and 2000). Herbert S. Parmet provides the fullest treatment of the elder George Bush in *George Bush: The Life of a Lone Star Yankee* (New York, 1997). The Clinton years have yet to enter the realm of history.

ACKNOWLEDGMENTS

The author would like to thank the various audiences on whom he has tested the arguments offered here. Their friendly criticism has been most helpful. Larisa Heimert and Jenya Weinreb of Yale University Press have been thoroughly professional; likewise the anonymous referees Ms. Heimert enlisted to read the manuscript. Jim Hornfischer of Literary Group International supplied his usual mix of intelligence and enthusiasm. Parts of chapter 4 appeared in *Critical Reflections on the Cold War,* edited by Martin J. Medhurst and H. W. Brands; thanks to Texas A&M University Press for permission to use that material.

Acheson, Dean, 63, 95–96
Adams, John, 4
Adams, Sam, 31
Affirmative action, 115
Afghanistan, 137–38
Africa, 80, 89
Agriculture Adjustment Act, 21, 23
Aid to Families with Dependent Children, 115
Alien Act (1798), 4
Alien Act (1918), 51
Amendment, Thirteenth, 33, 50
Amendment, Fourteenth, 33, 50
Amendment, Fifteenth, 33, 50
Amendment, Sixteenth, 38
American Civil Liberties Union, 43
American Protective League, 41

Antiwar movement (re Vietnam), 101–3
Arbenz, Jacobo, 72
Ayub Khan, Mohammad, 123

Baker, Newton, 35
Baker, Ray Stannard, 38
Ball, George, 123
Bank of the United States, 5
Baruch, Bernard, 37
Bay of Pigs invasion, 83
Biddle, Nicholas, 6
Bill of Rights, 4, 33
Bomb, atomic. *See* Weapons, nuclear
Brandt, Willy, 108
Brezhnev, Leonid, 111
Brezhnev doctrine, 157
Brown v. Board of Education of Topeka, 79, 112–15
Bryan, William Jennings, 10

Bureau of Internal Revenue, 31

Burleson, Albert Sidney, 40–41

Bush, George H. W., 160–61, 164

Bush, George W., 171–72

Calhoun, John C., 9

Cambodia, 105

Campaign to Re-elect the President, 120

Cannon, Lou, 139

Carnegie, Andrew, 9

Carswell, G. Harrold, 114

Carter, Jimmy, 127, 132–38

Casey, William, 143

Castro, Fidel, 82–83, 124, 160

Central America, 128, 143–44, 150. *See also individual countries*

Central Intelligence Agency (CIA), 60, 72, 124–25

Chase, Salmon, 30

Chiang Kai-shek, 64

China, 61, 64–65, 106–11, 117, 120

Civil rights, 79–82, 114

Civil Rights Act, 91

Civil War, 7–8, 30–34, 50

Civilian Conservation Corps, 23

Clark, Champ, 36–37

Clay, Henry, 5–6, 9

Clean Air Act, 113

Cleveland, Grover, 10

Clinton, Bill, vii, 154, 162–70

Cold War, x-xii, 54–70, 100–101, 123–25, 159–60

Commerce Department, 19

Committee on Public Information, 38

Communism (and Communists), 72–73, 80, 95–97, 140–41. *See also* China; Soviet Union

Congress, 2, 6; and Carter, 133–34; and Civil War, 30; and Cold War, 56–60; and Vietnam, 101, 105; and World War I, 35–36

Conscription, 31–32, 35–36

Conservatives, vii-viii; and Cold War, 57–61, 63–66; and Kennedy, 85–86

Continental Congress, 28–29

"Contract with America," 166–67

Contras (Nicaraguan), 143–44

Coolidge, Calvin, 19

Cost-of-living-allowances (COLAS), 116

Coughlin, Charles, 23

Council of Economic Advisers, 84

Covert operations, 71–72

Creel, George, 35, 38

Croly, Herbert, 13–14

Cuba, 82–83; and missile crisis, 83–84

De Gaulle, Charles, 108

Debs, Eugene, 41

Declaration of Independence, 28–29

Demobilization (after World War II), 51–52

Democrats, 8, 10, 67, 128–29, 147, 170; and Vietnam, 101

Department of Defense, 60, 85

Department of Education, 133

Department of Energy, 132–33

Depression, Great, 20–21

Détente, xii, 106–11, 142

Diem, Ngo Dinh, 96

Dole, Robert, 167

Donnelly, Ignatius, 9

Doolittle, James, 71–73

Dulles, Allen, 72

Dulles, John Foster, 71, 106–7

Eagleton, Thomas, 130

Education, federal aid to, 45–46, 78–79, 91

Eisenhower, Dwight, 67–82

Eisenhower, Edgar, 74–75

Elkins Act, 11

Ellsberg, Daniel, 118–19

Emancipation Proclamation, 33

Environmental Protection Agency, 113

Equal Employment Opportunity Commission, 115

Fair Deal, 67

Faubus, Orval, 80

Federal Agricultural Improvement and Reform Act, 171

Federal Bureau of Investigation, 118, 124

Federal Reserve System, 17–18

Federal Trade Commission, 17–18, 85

Federalists, 3–4

Ford, Gerald, 131, 134

Ford, Henry II, 113

"Four-minute men," 38
Fuchs, Klaus, 73
Fulbright, J. William, 102

Gallup poll, 24–25. *See also* Public opinion
Garment, Leonard, 112–13
Germany, 157–58
Gingrich, Newt, 166–67, 169
Glasnost, 157
Goldwater, Barry, ix, 96
Gorbachev, Mikhail, 153–58
Gore, Al, 171–72
Great Society, vii, 91–97
Gregory, Thomas, 41
Guatemala, 72
Gulf of Tonkin resolution, 96, 105
Gulf War, 160

Habeas corpus, 32
Haldeman, H. R., 117
Hamilton, Alexander, 3
Harding, Warren G., 19–20
Haynsworth, Clement, 114
Heller, Walter, 86
Helms, Richard, 100
Hepburn Act, 11
Hiss, Alger, 73

Ho Chi Minh, 99
Hobby, Oveta Culp, 78
Holmes, Oliver Wendell Jr., 43–44
Hoover, Herbert, 19–20
House, Edward, 37
Human rights, 135
Humphrey, Hubert, 103, 128–30
Hussein, Saddam, 160

Iacocca, Lee, 113
Ideology, in Cold War, 110–11
Internal Revenue Act (and Service), 18, 31
Interstate highway system, 76–77
Iran, 72, 136–37, 150
Iran-contra operation and scandal, 143, 149–50
Iraq, 160

Jackson, Andrew, 6–7, 30–31
Japanese-Americans, 43–44
Jefferson, Thomas, 4–7
Johnson, Lyndon, vii, ix, 68, 90–103
Justice Department, 41–42, 79–80, 85

Kennan, George, 54
Kennedy, John, 68, 82–91
Kennedy, Robert, 103, 130
Keynesianism, 87–88, 147
Khomeini, Ayatollah, 136–37
Khrushchev, Nikita, 83, 88
Kim Il Sung, 63
King, Martin Luther Jr., 79
Kissinger, Henry, 108, 122, 130
Knox, Philander, 11
Korea (and Korean War), 63–65, 70
Kuwait, 160

Le Duc Tho, 122
Lease, Mary, 9
Lebanon, 144
Legal Tender Act, 30
LeMay, Curtis, 102
Liberalism, and Cold War, x, 67–97; 172–74, 176; death of, vii, 127–28, 150–51; definition of, viii; future of, 176–77; and positive state, 18; and public opinion, ix-xi; and Vietnam, 131. *See also* Eisenhower, Kennedy, Johnson, Nixon, Carter

Lincoln, Abraham, 30–33
Lincoln, James, 3
Literary Digest, 24
Lodge, Henry Cabot, 80
Long, Huey, 23
Luce, Henry, 64
Lumumba, Patrice, 124

MacArthur, Douglas, 65
Madison, James, 3–4, 7
Magna Carta, 3
Manhattan project, 46
Mao Zedong, 61, 108
Marshall, George, 56
Marshall plan, 56–57
Martin, Luther, 3
Martin, Thomas, 35
McCarthy, Eugene, 102–3, 130
McCarthy, Joseph, 64–65
McGovern, George, 102, 129–31
McKinley, William, 9–10
McNamara, Robert, 85
Medicaid, 91, 115
Medicare, 91, 148
Middle East, 89. *See also individual countries*
Mondale, Walter, ix

Morgan, J. P., 9–11
Mosadeq, Mohammed, 72

National Banking Act, 30–31
National Defense Education
    Act, 79
National Recovery Administra-
    tion, 21
National Road, 6
National Security Council, 60
"Negative income tax," 115
Nelson, Donald, 44
Neoconservatism (and neo-
    conservatives), 127, 136–37,
    141–45
Neutralism, 106–7
New Deal, 1, 21–26, 67–68
New Federalism, 112–13
New Left, 101
New Look, 70–71, 74
New York Times, 117–18
Newlands Act, 17–18
Nicaragua, 136
Nixon, Richard, xii, 100–125,
    131–34, 155
North Atlantic Treaty (and
    NATO), 58–60, 65
Northern Securities Company,
    11
NSC-68, 61–63, 75

O'Brian, John Lord, 42
Occupational Safety and
    Health (OSHA), 115
Office of Civilian Defense, 43
Office of Scientific Research
    and Development, 46
Office of War Information, 42–
    43, 50–51
Office of War Mobilization, 42
Oil, 132–33

Paine, Thomas, 2
Palmer, A. Mitchell, 51
Panama Canal treaties, 136
Pentagon Papers, 117
Perestroika, 157
Perot, H. Ross, 164
Personal Responsibility and
    Work Opportunity Recon-
    ciliation Act, 171
"Philadelphia plan," 115
Phillips, Wendell, 33
Pinchot, Amos, 36
Pinchot, Gifford, 12
"Plumbers," 118–20
Populism, 9–10, 26
Presley, Elvis, vii
Progressivism, 10–18, 26
Public opinion, 1; and Bush
    (George H. W.), 161; and

Carter, 138; and Congress, 165, 168; and Kennedy, 83–84; and Reagan, 148
Public Works Administration, 23
Pure Food and Drug Act, 12

Reagan, Ronald, ix, 127–28, 138–57
Reconstruction, 50
Reed, Thomas, 9
Republicans, 8–12, 20, 101, 147, 165–70
Republicans (Jeffersonian), 4
Research, scientific, 46–47
Revolution, American (and Revolutionary War), 2, 27–30, 49
Rockefeller, John D., 9
Roosevelt, Franklin, 20–26, 43–45, 175
Roosevelt, Theodore, 11–16, 18–19, 36, 41, 175
Rosenberg, Julius and Ethel, 73

SALT (Strategic Arms Limitation Talks, and Treaties), 117–18, 136, 154–55
Schechter case, 22
Sedition Act (1798), 4

Sedition Act (1918), 51
Shah of Iran, 72
Sherman Antitrust Act, 11
Shriver, Sargent, 130
Shultz, George, 115
"Sinatra doctrine," 157
Sinclair, Upton, 12
Social Security, 23–26, 67–68, 75–76, 116, 148, 171
Soviet Union, 53–57, 61, 70–71, 140–41; and Afghanistan, 137–38; and détente, 106–11, 120; dissolution of, 158
Space race, 88–90
Spanish-American War, 34
Spaulding, Elbridge, 30
Spies, 72–73
Sputnik, 78
St. Lawrence seaway, 76
Stalin, Joseph, 53
Starr, Kenneth, 170
Stevenson, Adlai, 68
Stockman, David, 149
Strategic Defense Initiative (SDI), 146
Sukarno, 123
Supplemental Security Income program, 116
Supreme Court, 11, 22, 25

Taft, Robert, 57–61, 65–68

Taft, William Howard, 12–13

Taney, Roger, 32

Tarbell, Ida, 38

Taxes, 17, 28, 38–40, 86–87, 147

Tet offensive, 100, 102–3

Thatcher, Margaret, 158

Thieu, Nguyen Van, 121

Tocqueville, Alexis de, 6–8

Townshend, Charles, 2

Truman, Harry, 54–56, 64, 95–96

Truman doctrine, 54–56

United Nations, 52–53, 80

United States Housing Authority, 45

United States Steel Corporation, 84

Vallandigham, Clement, 32

Van Buren, Martin, 6

Van Hise, Charles, 14

Vandenberg, Arthur, 60

Versailles treaty, 19

Vietnam (and Vietnam War), xi–xii, 84–85, 95–106, 119–23, 128–29, 172

"Vietnamization," 103–4

Volstead Act, 51

Voting Rights Act, 91

Wagner Act, 67

Walpole, Robert, 2

War Industries Board, 36–37, 50–51

War Labor Board, 42, 44

War on Poverty, 91–92

War Powers Resolution, 121

War Production Board, 42, 44

Washington, George, 2, 28

Watergate scandal, 117–23, 130, 172–73

Weapons, nuclear (and arms race), 46, 69–71, 75, 144–47, 153–57, 160–61. *See also* SALT

Webster, Daniel, 9

Welfare, 171

White, William Allen, 22

Wilson, Charles, 74–75

Wilson, Woodrow, 13–19, 34–42, 175

Witte, Edwin, 44

Works Progress Administration, 23

World War I, 17, 19, 34–42, 50–51

World War II, 42–47, 51–52

Yalta agreement, 53